Just as every seed planted carries the potential to grow into something extraordinary, this book represents years of learning, growing, and sharing — rooted in passion and brought life to one plant at a time.

This book was written to inspire, educate, and empower anyone who has ever looked at a piece of land, or a simple pot on a porch, and wondered what could grow there. The knowledge shared here is meant to be used, applied, and passed on. But the words themselves belong to the one who wrote them.

For permission requests, speaking engagements, or wholesale inquiries, visit: rootedinjs.com

The information in this book is provided for educational and inspirational purposes. While every effort has been made to ensure accuracy, growing conditions vary and results may differ. The author assumes no liability for outcomes resulting from the application of information contained in this work. Always consult local agricultural guidelines for your specific region.

ISBN: 979-8-9952819-0-0

Published by Rooted In J's Library

rootedinjs.com

Table of Contents

Table of Contents

Table of Contents

Friendly Note

The information shared in this book is based on my personal gardening experience, research, and knowledge passed down through family members and fellow growers. It is provided for educational and informational purposes only and should not be considered professional medical, agricultural, or gardening advice.

Many plants mentioned in this book are traditionally used in cooking, cultural practices, or home remedies. If you plan to use any plant for health-related purposes, especially if you are pregnant, nursing, taking medication, or managing a medical condition, please consult with a qualified healthcare professional before doing so.

Gardening results can vary depending on soil conditions, climate, pests, growing methods, and many other factors outside the author's control. By using the information in this book, you accept full responsibility for your own gardening decisions and outcomes.

The author makes no guarantees regarding results and is not responsible for any loss, injury, or damages that may occur from the use or misuse of the information provided in this book.

How This Book Started

Just as every seed planted carries the potential to grow into something extraordinary, this book represents years of learning, growing, and sharing — rooted in passion and brought life to one plant at a time.

This book grew out of a simple idea. What if I could introduce people to one new plant every day for thirty days? I called it my Thirty Day Garden Challenge, and each day I shared a plant you could actually grow here in Florida — along with the real-life stories, tips, and mistakes I had learned along the way.

What happened surprised me. People did not just follow along. They asked questions, shared their own gardens, and kept coming back wanting more. That challenge became a movement in my little corner of the internet. But I did not want it to live online only. That is why this book exists.

What you are holding now is the expanded edition. Version one introduced 30+ plants. This version grows with me, and with you, adding more plants as I discover, test, and fall in love with them. Consider this your invitation to experience them with me as they come.

You do not have to know anything about the challenge to use this book. Each plant stands completely on its own, with full growing instructions, personal stories, kitchen tips, and the kind of guidance I wish I had when I started. Think of it as a Florida gardening crash course in book form — whether you are flipping straight to your favorite plant or reading cover to cover.

Let me be clear right up front: this is not your everyday tomato and lettuce kind of gardening book. The plants in these pages are the ones that thrive in Florida's unique climate, bring unexpected flavors to your kitchen, and give you a garden that feels alive and abundant year-round. No fancy jargon. No fluff. No one telling you to buy fifteen things you do not need.

For those who joined me during the challenge — this is the deeper dive, the polished version, the place where everything we learned together comes full circle. And for those who are brand new? Welcome. This book was written to help you grow with confidence, wherever you are starting from.

HOW TO USE THIS BOOK

Follow the Planting Times — Each plant includes a Best Planting Time based on Florida's unique growing seasons. Planting at the right time is half the battle.

Start With What You Eat — Got Kids Who Inhale Bananas? Start there. The best garden is one that fits your family and your table.

Small Space? No Problem — Each plant notes whether it grows well in containers. Whether you have a patio, a balcony, or a sunny patch, there is something here for you.

Use the Did You Know and Kitchen Tip Sections — Quick tips that go beyond the garden and into the kitchen. Juice it, bake it, brew it, or toss it in dinner. You are growing flavor and function.

Learn From the Stories — Every plant page includes a story, lesson, or memory from real experience. Let those stories save you time, money, and a few tears.

Discover the Benefits — From roots to leaves, many of these plants carry health benefits you did not even know you needed.

My Why…

People think gardening is just about vegetables, but for us, it is about the food we grew up with. In my family, papaya is not just a fruit you eat for breakfast. It is legim[1]. It is green papaya cooked down slowly and seasoned heavily with epis[2], garlic, and thyme. It is the food the women in my family made to feed the whole house without ever using a measuring spoon. When I grow papaya today, I am growing the food I want my kids to know.

So, when we began gardening, it was not because we were trying to have an aesthetic backyard. We were trying to reclaim something we did not want to lose. We were tired of buying fruit that did not taste like fruit. We were tired of paying ten dollars for blueberries that disappeared in the car before we got home. We were tired of food that felt like it had no story.

But there is more to it than that.

When my husband and I got married, we decided to leave Hollywood, Florida and expand our lives. We moved to West Central Florida, somewhere between Tampa and Orlando, where the beach was no longer our backyard, and our neighbors had cows and horses instead of condos. For a city girl who grew up with boardwalk weekends at Margaritaville listening to live bands and fresh oysters at Gigi's, it was culture shock.

No more ocean breeze. No more walking out the door and feeling that salt air cools you down. Just heat. And space. And quiet that felt too big.

So, we decided to bring the oasis to us.

We started planting. Not because we knew what we were doing, but because we needed something that felt like ours in a place that still felt foreign. What began as a hobby, just trying to make the yard feel less empty, grew into something bigger. A food forest. A space where we could walk outside and pick fruit the way we used to walk to the market for seafood.

---

[1] Legim is a Haitian eggplant stew that is served as a side along with rice, plantains, and meat or fish. Sometimes Legim is made as a one-pot dish cooked with braised meat.

[2] Haitian epis is a foundational, savory green seasoning paste made from blended peppers, garlic, herbs, and aromatics, serving as the primary marinade and flavor base for most Haitian dishes.

But it did not start that way. We moved plants three or four times because we planted them in the wrong spot. We bought trees that had no business in Central Florida for heat. Peach trees varieties that need cold winters we do not have. Things that looked good at the garden store but died two months later. The amount of money we wasted? Lord, my grandma would not be happy.

She grew up in Haiti, where you did not waste anything. Where every seed had a purpose and every plant fed somebody. She would have looked at my dead peach tree and shaken her head.

But we kept going. Because we were not just planting a garden. We were planting a life in a place that did not feel like home yet. And somewhere along the way, between the failures and the fruit trees that actually survived, it started to work.

The yard that felt too big started to feel like ours. The heat that felt unbearable started to make sense once we learned how to work with it instead of against it. And the garden that started as something to fill the space became the thing that feeds us, grounds us, and reminds us why we stayed.

Our garden is not a hobby. It is our table. Our rhythm. Our way of slowing life down enough to remember who we are.

The Quiet Provision

When I step outside, I am reminded that things grow slow and still become something. That fruit does not rush itself. That seasons do not apologize for taking time. Gardening became a mirror for the rest of my life. Patience. Presence. Provision. All happening quietly, under the soil.

Find a quiet moment today, even if it is two minutes while washing dishes or sitting in the car before going inside. Ask yourself: What foods feel like home to me?

Write down five of them. Do not think hard. Do not decorate the list. Whatever comes first is what your garden wants to grow.

My Why…

Figure 1 Our Backyard before a single fruit tree

Chapter 1: Before You Plant a Thing

Let me start here. I do not garden because I have endless free time. I have a full-time corporate job that keeps me in meetings and emails, little kids who seem to run on rocket fuel, a house that always has one more thing to fix or clean, and a husband who is right there in the thick of it with me. He has been in this since the beginning, building beds, hauling soil, and planting trees. This is something we both poured into for our family.

The truth is, sometimes all I get is five minutes outside. Five minutes between a call and cooking dinner. Five minutes before the kids run out, or the baby wakes up. And those five minutes are everything. I walk outside, see what is growing, and it reminds me why we do this. We are not just planting for looks. We are planting for meals, for our kids, for the small wins that keep us moving.

It matters to my husband, Jermaine, just as much. He even wrote a book called, "Grow Food NOT Lawns: Simple Steps To Turn Any Yard Into A Year-Round Garden", because that is what we believe. Why waste space on grass when the same ground can feed your family all year?

Figure 2 – How it started, Our 1st Garden

The Heat I Thought I Knew

Now let me tell you something nobody warns you about when you move from Miami to Central Florida.

Chapter 1: Before You Plant a Thing

I grew up in Miami. I know heat. I know humidity. I know what it feels like when the air is so thick you could drink it. But Miami heat has the ocean right there. You get a breeze. The water cools things down just enough. Eighty-five degrees in Miami feels different because the air moves, because you are near water, because shade actually works.

Central Florida? No ocean. No breeze. No relief.

The sun just sits on you. On your plants. On the soil. It does not move. Eighty-five degrees here feel like a hundred in Miami because there is nothing to cut it. The heat does not come and go. It stays. All day. Every day. And if you do not understand that difference, your plants will tell you real quick.

I thought I knew Florida. Turns out, I knew Miami. Central Florida had other plans. On the coast, you get a natural cooling engine called a sea breeze. As the land heats up during the day, the hot air rises. The cooler, heavier air sitting over the ocean rushes in to fill the empty space, creating that constant wind. Inland, we are just too far away for that cycle to reach us effectively. Instead of rising and being replaced by cool ocean air, our hot and humid air simply sits in place. That stagnant pressure acts like a lid, trapping the heat directly at ground level where your roots are trying to survive.

The Expensive Education

This is the part that hit me hardest once I started digging. When you're in Miami, the breeze is like a built-in safety net; it dries the leaves, moves the pests along, and keeps the soil from turning into a swamp or a brick. But here, inland? That stagnant, heavy air turns every container and every row of dirt into a pressure cooker. You aren't just gardening against the bugs or the soil quality; you are gardening against a system that never cools down. It's a constant, low-grade stress on the plants that I wasn't equipped to manage. And that, I learned, is where the trouble starts.

Of course, it was not all smooth. Gardening humbled me quick.

People always say the easiest thing to grow is tomatoes. And I just want to know, WHO ARE THESE PEOPLE? Because it was not me. Tomatoes and I had beef in Florida. They did not like me, or maybe I did not like them. The moment I thought I had them figured out, boom, the leaves looked sick. Yellow spots, curling, bugs having a picnic on them. Every time I thought I was about to harvest a handful, the plant laughed in my face.

At one point I was at the garden store so much, the cashiers probably thought I worked there. I was buying sprays, soils, gadgets, anything they claimed would fix my tomato troubles. And still, nothing. By the end of one season I had three lonely tomatoes, a beat-up pepper that looked like it had been in a fight, and carrots I swear disappeared into another dimension.

I had an app on my phone to diagnose sick plants. I watched YouTube videos until my eyes hurt. I Googled *"why are my plants dying"* so many times I am surprised Google did not just send me a sympathy card.

None of it worked.

Because here is what nobody tells you: the internet gives you general advice. It does not know you are in Central Florida, not near the coast, planting in sand that used to be a beach, watering plants that are cooking in heat with no ocean breeze to save them.

That is when it hit me: I had to stop. Stop letting these plants tell me what to do. Stop throwing money into the ground for the sake of looking like a gardener. Gardening is supposed to feed you, not boss you around.

The Switch That Changed Everything

So, I switched gears. Instead of planting what looked good on a seed packet, I started planting what actually worked in my area, and more importantly, what my kiddos actually eat. Because let's be real, what is the point of growing a perfect head of lettuce if nobody in your house eats salad?

That switch changed everything. Suddenly my garden stopped feeling like a science experiment gone wrong and started feeling like part of our daily life. The harvests matched our meals. The kids got excited to pick fruits and veggies they actually liked. And I stopped wasting time and money trying to be the tomato whisperer.

The Lie the Garden Store Told Me

Here is what I wish someone had pulled me aside and whispered in my ear before I spent hundreds of dollars at the garden center:

Just because they sell it does not mean you can grow it.

I used to walk into Home Depot or Lowe's and think, "Well, they're selling it in Florida, so it must work in Florida." Made sense, right? Why would they stock apple trees if apple trees don't belong here? Why would they have tomato plants sitting out in May if May is the wrong time to plant tomatoes?

Turns out, the garden store does not care about your zip code. They care about selling plants.

They sell the same seed racks in Florida that they sell in Georgia, California, North Carolina. They stock whatever corporate says to stock. And corporate does not know about your sandy soil, your inland heat, or the fact that Central Florida in July will murder a lettuce plant by lunchtime.

I learned this the expensive way.

I bought apple trees because they were on sale. Turns out, apples need cold winter hours we do not have in Central Florida. Those trees just sat there, confused, waiting for a winter that was never going to come.

I bought tomato plants in May because the shelf was full of them. Big, green, healthy-looking plants with little yellow flowers already starting. I thought, "Perfect! Head start!" What I did not know was that May in Central Florida is basically plant murder season for tomatoes. The heat does not let them set fruit. The humidity invites every disease. I would have been better off waiting until fall.

I bought lettuce seeds with a picture on the packet that said "Grow Year-Round!" In Florida, summer lettuce does not grow. It wilts, bolts, and turns into mush before you can even make a salad.

Nobody at the store told me any of this. And why would they? They get paid when you buy the plant, not when it actually grows.

What I Should Have Been Asking

So instead of grabbing whatever looked good on the shelf, I started asking different questions:

Not "Does this plant look healthy?" but "Does this plant belong in Central Florida heat, zone 10a, actually?"

Not "Is this on sale?" but "Is this the right season to plant it?"

Not "Will my kids eat this?" (okay, I still ask that one) but "Can this actually survive here, or am I throwing money into the ground?"

Once I stopped trusting the garden store to tell me what works, I started looking at what actually thrives here without babysitting. What my neighbors who have been here for twenty years are growing. What the old Haitian and Caribbean families in the area plant in their yards. What grows wild and unbothered in Florida heat.

That is when my garden stopped being a graveyard and started being a food source.

Watch Your Yard Before You Buy a Single Plant

Nobody tells you this, and it's just as important as knowing what to grow: you have to know *where* to put it. Before you spend a single dollar at the garden center, you need to watch your yard the way you watch people. Where is it gentle? Where is it harsh? Where does the sun sit and refuse to leave?

Go stand outside for two minutes. Don't bring a plant. Don't bring a plan. Just stand there.

Watch where the morning light touches first. That is your sweet spot. That morning sun gives your plants the energy they need to grow without cooking them alive. Now, look for where that afternoon sun camps out and refuses to quit. That's your danger zone.

And don't treat shade like the enemy. In Florida, shade is mercy. Your plants need a break from that intensity, especially when the day hits its peak.

But here is the thing most people miss: notice where the heat *bounces*. If you have a driveway, a concrete patio, or a light-colored wall, the sun isn't just hitting your plants from above—it's reflecting off those surfaces and cooking them from the side. It heats up the ground and holds that temperature long after the sun goes down. Your plants aren't just dealing with the sky; they're dealing with an oven that never turns off.

Once you learn your yard's patterns, you've got your map. And once you have the map, the rest of this whole gardening thing is just finding your rhythm and having the patience to stick with it.

Truth Moment

A plant that looks dead in the afternoon may be perfectly healthy. Some plants fold their leaves to protect themselves. If it perks back up in the evening or the next morning, it is fine.

But if it looks cooked at 8 a.m.? That plant is telling you it wants a little shade. Listen. Do not fight it. Plants will tell you the truth if you stop trying to garden by pride.

Garden Reflection

Step outside today. Stand in your yard or on your patio for two minutes. Do not touch anything. Just observe.

- Where does the morning sun touch first?
- Where does shade fall in the afternoon?

• Where does the heat bounce off your house or driveway and hit twice?

Write it down. This is your planting map. Nothing grows well without you knowing this first.

Chapter 2: Soil, Sun & Water

Soil: The Foundation You Cannot Fake

Your Yard Used to Be the Ocean

When I first started, I thought dirt was dirt. Dig a hole, drop in a plant, call it a day. Florida taught me quick that not all soil is created equal.

Here is what nobody tells you when you move to Central Florida:

Your backyard was underwater 2.5 million years ago.

I am not talking poetic. I am talking literal. The spot where you are trying to grow tomatoes? That was the Gulf of Mexico. The place you want to plant fruit trees? Ocean floor.

Florida was completely submerged for most of its geological history. The last time the whole state was underwater was about 2.5 to 4.5 million years ago. [3]

Even during the ice ages, when sea levels dropped 400 feet and Florida was twice as wide as it is now, Central Florida was still dealing with what the ocean left behind.

What the ocean left behind is limestone. Hundreds, sometimes thousands of feet of limestone underneath your yard. All of it made from the compressed bodies of tiny marine creatures that lived and died and piled up for millions of years. That is your foundation.

On top of that limestone? A thin layer of sand. Sand that washed down from the Appalachian Mountains over millions of years and got deposited across Florida as the seas rose and fell.

---

[3] For those interested in the 'why' behind our sandy soil: The Florida Museum of Natural History notes that Florida was almost entirely submerged during the Pliocene epoch, roughly 2.5 to 4.5 million years ago. That history defines exactly why our 'dirt' drains so fast.

That sand is what you are trying to garden in.

Figure 3 Our Backyard Sandy Soil

Not topsoil. Not the rich, dark, crumbly stuff that builds up in forests over thousands of years. Sand. Beach sand. Playground sand. The kind that holds zero nutrients and lets water run through it like a broken cup.

When you dig a hole in your yard and hit that white, gritty layer six inches down, that is not dirt. That is geological history telling you that you are not working with soil. You are working with what used to be a beach.

Why This Matters for Your Plants

Plants need three things from soil:

1. Nutrients - to grow and produce
2. Water retention - so roots can drink without drowning
3. Structure - so roots can breathe, stretch, and anchor

Florida sand gives you none of these.

Sand has no nutrients. Water runs straight through it. And the "structure" is just loose grains that shift and compact and heat up like a stove when the sun hits it.

So when you plant a tomato in pure Florida sand and it dies three weeks later, it is not because you did not water enough. It is because you tried to grow food in what is essentially a beach.

You are not gardening. You are trying to create soil where none exists.

The Bag Scam: What They Are Really Selling You

So you go to the garden store. You need soil. The bags are lined up, all claiming to be "garden soil" or "potting mix" or "planting mix." You grab a few, haul them home, and start filling pots or raised beds.

Here is what I wish someone had told me before I spent hundreds of dollars on bags:

Half of what is in that bag is filler.

Reading the Fine Print

Turn the bag over. Look at the ingredients list. This is where the scam lives.

I used to buy Miracle-Gro Garden Soil because it was cheap and available everywhere. The bag said "feeds plants for up to 3 months!" which sounded great.

Then I read the ingredients:

- Processed forest products
- Peat moss
- Fertilizer

Sounds legit, right?

Wrong.

"Processed forest products" is code for wood chips that have not broken down yet. They are not compost. They are not aged. They are just ground-up wood taking up space in the bag. And as they break down in your soil, they actually steal nitrogen from your plants to fuel the decomposition process.

So you are paying $8 for a bag that is maybe 40% actual growing medium and 60% wood chunks that are actively working against you.

What Good Soil Actually Looks Like

Compare that to FoxFarm Happy Frog Potting Soil.

Ingredients:

- Aged forest products
- sphagnum peat moss
- perlite
- earthworm castings

- bat guano
- humic acid
- mycorrhizae

See the difference?

"Aged forest products" means the wood has already broken down into humus. It is stable. It is not going to steal nitrogen.

Earthworm castings = actual nutrients. Bat guano = actual nutrients. Mycorrhizae [4]= beneficial fungi that help roots absorb nutrients.

This bag costs $18 instead of $8. But you are getting soil that actually works instead of filler with a fertilizer coating.

The Real Cost

If you are planting 50+ plants, you are going to need a lot of soil.

Let's say you are filling ten 5-gallon containers. That is 50 gallons of soil.

Option 1: Miracle-Gro Garden Soil

- $8 per 1.5 cubic foot bag (roughly 11 gallons)
- You need 5 bags = $40
- But half of it is filler, so you are really only getting 25 gallons of usable soil
- You will need to add compost[5], worm castings, and fertilizer separately = another $30-50

Total: $70-90

Option 2: Happy Frog Potting Soil

- $18 per 2 cubic foot bag (roughly 15 gallons)

---

[4] Mycorrhizae (pronounced *my-cor-RYE-zee*) are beneficial fungi that live in your soil and form a partnership with your plant roots. It is a mutually beneficial trade: the plant gives the fungi sugars (energy), and in exchange, the fungi act like a massive, microscopic extension cord that reaches out into the soil to grab water and nutrients for the plant.

[5] Compost is the nutrient-rich, dark "black gold" created by letting kitchen scraps and yard waste naturally break down over time. Think of it as a long-term savings account for your soil that acts like a sponge to hold moisture and food for your plants' roots.

- You need 4 bags = $72
- Everything you need is already in the bag

Total: $72

So the "cheap" soil ends up costing just as much once you fix it. And you still spent hours amending it.

Or you skip the cheap soil entirely and make your own.

Should You Buy in Bulk?

This is where people get tricked.

You see bulk soil advertised: "Only $35 per cubic yard delivered!"

A cubic yard is 27 cubic feet, which is about 200 gallons. That sounds like a steal compared to buying bags.

When Bulk Makes Sense

Buy bulk if:

- ✓ You are filling large raised beds (4x8 or bigger)
- ✓ You are amending a large in-ground area
- ✓ You can pick it up yourself (delivery fees kill the savings)
- ✓ You are willing to screen it and amend it yourself

For example, if you are building three 4x8 raised beds that are 12 inches deep, you need about 1 cubic yard of soil. Buying that in bags would cost $200-300. Buying bulk for $35-50 and amending it yourself saves you real money.

When Bulk Does Not Make Sense

Do not buy bulk if:

- ❖ You are filling containers (bulk soil is too heavy and compacts in pots)
- ❖ You only need a few bags worth
- ❖ You do not have a way to move/screen/amend it
- ❖ Delivery costs more than $50 (at that point, just buy bags)

I learned this the hard way. I ordered a cubic yard of "garden soil" for $45 delivered. It showed up in my driveway as a mountain of clay-heavy dirt with sticks and rocks mixed in. I spent two weekends screening it, mixing in compost and perlite, and hauling it to my beds in a wheelbarrow.

I saved maybe $30. But I lost an entire weekend.

For containers? Always buy bagged or make your own. For raised beds? Bulk can work if you are willing to do the labor.

The DIY Soil Recipes That Actually Work

Once I stopped trusting the bags and stopped trying to buy my way out of bad soil, I started making my own.

Here is what I use. These are not fancy. They are not complicated. They work.

For Containers (5-gallon pots, grow bags, etc.)

Toni's Container Mix:

- 40% coco coir (or peat moss)
- 30% compost
- 20% perlite
- 10% worm castings

This mix is light enough that it does not compact in pots, but heavy enough that it holds water and nutrients. The perlite [6] keeps it from getting waterlogged. The worm castings feed your plants without burning them.

Cost breakdown:

- Coco coir brick (expands to 2.5 cubic feet): $8
- Compost (2 cubic feet): $6
- Perlite (2 cubic feet): $10
- Worm castings (1 cubic foot): $12

---

[6] Perlite is that lightweight, white volcanic glass you see mixed into potting soil that looks like little bits of Styrofoam. It is added to container mixes to create air pockets, which prevents the soil from compacting and helps excess water drain away quickly so your plant roots don't suffocate.

Total for about 6 cubic feet of mix: $36

Compare that to buying 6 cubic feet of Happy Frog at $54. You just saved $18 AND you know exactly what is in it.

For Raised Beds

- 50% bulk topsoil (screened)
- 30% compost
- 20% peat moss or coco coir

Raised beds can handle heavier soil than containers because the roots have more room to spread. You want something that holds moisture but still drains.

Cost for a 4x8 bed, 12 inches deep (about 1 cubic yard):

- Bulk topsoil (half a yard): $20-25
- Compost (10 bags, 2 cubic feet each): $60
- Peat moss (3 large bales): $30

Total: $110-115

Buying bagged soil for the same bed would cost $250-300. You just saved $150.

For In-Ground Planting (fruit trees, perennials[7])

You are not filling a whole bed. You are just amending the soil in the planting hole.

Toni's In-Ground Amendment:

- Dig a hole twice as wide and just as deep as the root ball
- Mix the dirt you dug out with 50% compost
- Add a handful of worm castings
- Backfill around the plant

Cost per tree: About $3-5 in compost and castings.

---

[7] A **perennial** is simply a plant that lives for more than two years.

Do NOT dig the hole and fill it with pure bagged soil. The roots will hit that "wall" where the good soil ends and the native sand begins, and they will just circle around inside the hole instead of spreading out. You want to encourage roots to grow INTO the native soil, so you amend the native soil instead of replacing it.

Where to Get Soil Ingredients for Free (or Cheap)

This is where you save real money.

1. Free Coffee Grounds (Starbucks)

Walk into any Starbucks and ask if they have used coffee grounds. Most locations keep them in bags behind the counter specifically for gardeners. They are free. You just take them.

Coffee grounds are nitrogen-rich and great for compost. I add them to my raised beds in the fall and let them break down over the winter.

Cost: $0

2. Free Rain Barrels (Hillsborough County)

Hillsborough County (and some other Florida counties) give away free rain barrels to residents. You just sign up online, show up at the distribution event, and take home a 55-gallon barrel with a spigot already installed.

I have three. They save me from using city water for my garden, and during rainy season they stay full.

Cost: $0 (normally $80-120 each)

3. Free Mulch (ChipDrop.com)

Arborists need to get rid of wood chips after trimming trees. ChipDrop connects them with people who want free mulch.

You sign up, they drop 10-20 cubic yards of wood chips in your driveway when a job is nearby. No charge.

The catch: You do not get to pick when it shows up, and it is A LOT of mulch. Like, a small mountain. And it is whatever they were chipping that day, so sometimes it is pine, sometimes it is oak, sometimes it is mixed.

But if you need mulch for paths, around trees, or to top-dress beds, this is unbeatable.

Cost: $0 (you can tip the driver $20 if you want, but it is not required)

Warning: Do NOT use fresh wood chips directly in your vegetable beds. Let them age for 6-12 months first, or use them only as a top layer on paths. Fresh chips steal nitrogen as they break down.

4. Cheap Compost (Municipal Sources)

Many cities and counties in Florida have compost facilities where they turn yard waste into compost and sell it cheap.

In Hillsborough County, you can get bulk compost for $10-15 per cubic yard if you pick it up yourself. That is a fraction of what bagged compost costs.

Call your local solid waste department and ask if they sell compost. Most do.

Cost: $10-15 per cubic yard (vs. $60-100 in bags)

Water: You Cannot Water Your Way Out of Bad Soil

Let me tell you about the summer I got a warning from the city.

We had just planted seven fruit trees in May. Yes, May. In Central Florida. I already told you that was a mistake. But I did not know that yet.

The trees were wilting. Every afternoon, they looked like they were dying. Leaves drooping, stems sagging, the whole plant just giving up.

So I watered. Every morning. Every evening. Sometimes at lunchtime if I could sneak outside between meetings.

I soaked those trees. I gave them everything I had.

And they still looked terrible.

Then I got a notice in the mail from the city: "Your water usage is significantly higher than normal. Please check for leaks or reduce usage to avoid additional charges."

I was watering so much, the city thought I had a broken pipe.

Here is what I did not understand: You cannot water your way out of bad soil.

The Problem Was Not the Water

The problem was the soil.

I had planted those trees in pure sand. No compost. No amendments. Just dug a hole, dropped the tree in, and backfilled with the same sand I pulled out.

That sand did not hold water. It did not hold nutrients. It did not hold anything.

Every time I watered, the water ran straight through the sand and down into the limestone below. The roots never got a chance to drink. By the time the sun came up, the soil was bone dry again.

So I kept watering. And the city kept sending me warnings.

What Actually Worked

I finally figured it out when I dug up one of the trees to move it. (Yes, I moved it. Three times. But that is another story.)

The soil around the roots was dry. Not damp. Not moist. Dust.

That is when it clicked.

The issue was not how much I was watering. The issue was that the soil had no ability to hold the water I was giving it.

I amended the soil. Mixed in compost, aged manure, coco coir[8]. Anything that would act like a sponge and hold moisture.

Then I watered deep, once every few days instead of shallow every day. Let the water soak all the way down. Let the roots chase it.

The trees perked up within two weeks.

And my water bill went back to normal.

The Lesson

If your plants are wilting and you are watering every day, the problem is probably not the watering schedule.

It is the soil.

Fix the soil first. Then worry about water.

Because no amount of water is going to save a plant that is sitting in sand.

The Truth About Florida Sun

Now let's talk about the third piece: sun.

---

[8] Coco coir is a byproduct made from the fibrous husks of coconuts that acts as an excellent, sustainable alternative to peat moss in potting mixes

I already told you in Chapter 1 that Central Florida sun is different from Miami sun. No ocean breeze. No relief. Just heat that sits and does not move.

But here is what I did not tell you:

The sun does not just hit your plants from above. It hits them from below.

Soil Temperature vs. Air Temperature

When the weather report says it is 95 degrees, they are talking about air temperature in the shade, measured five feet off the ground.

Your soil? It is hotter.

Sandy soil heats up fast. On a 95-degree day, the soil surface can hit 120-130 degrees. The top few inches where your plant roots live? Easily 110-115 degrees.

At that temperature, roots stop working. They cannot absorb water. They cannot absorb nutrients. They just try to survive.

That is why your plants wilt in the afternoon even when the soil is wet. The roots are too hot to function.

Mulch Is Not Optional

This is why I keep hammering mulch.

Mulch does not just keep weeds down. It does not just look nice.

Mulch keeps the soil cool.

A 2-3 inch layer of mulch can drop soil temperature by 10-15 degrees. That is the difference between roots that are cooked and roots that are working.

I used to think mulch was something you did to make your garden look finished. Now I know it is survival.

Bare soil in Florida is a death sentence.

The Toni Pledge

Repeat after me:

I pledge to build living soil, not buy dead dirt.

I pledge to mulch like my plants depend on it. (Because they do.)

I pledge to water deep, not often.

Garden Reflection

Go outside. Grab a handful of your soil.

Squeeze it. Does it hold together? Or does it fall apart like sand?

If it falls apart, you have work to do.

Write down one thing you can do this week to improve your soil. Add compost. Top-dress with mulch. Mix in some worm castings.

Just one thing.

Soil does not fix itself overnight. But every little bit you add makes it better.

Chapter 3: Grow Where You Are

(And How to Survive Florida's Mood Swings)

When people think about starting a garden, they picture a perfect setup. Raised beds lined in rows. A greenhouse. Drip irrigation. A compost system that looks like it has a membership card.

But that is not where most of us start. And thank God for that. Growth does not need perfection. It needs commitment.

Let me tell you what I learned the long way. You do not need a yard to begin. You do not need matching pots. You do not need every tool at the store. You do not even need to feel ready.

You start with one space. You start with one plant your family will actually eat. You start with one quiet decision to feed your home from your hands.

Because the truth is this: Where you live is already enough.

Why I Love Containers in Funky Florida Weather

Florida weather is chaos.

It is 85 degrees on Monday. By Thursday, it is 35 and your plants are shocked. Then two weeks later, it is back to 90 and everything is confused.

Hurricanes roll through in September. Freak cold snaps hit in January. Heat waves cook everything in July.

If your plants are stuck in the ground, they take whatever Florida throws at them. And sometimes, they lose.

But if your plants are in containers? You can move them.

Containers are your insurance policy.

When a cold front is coming, I move my tender tropicals to the south wall of the house where the brick radiates heat and the roof blocks frost. When a hurricane is forecast, I cluster everything against the house or move the smaller pots into the garage. When the summer sun is brutal, I shift containers into the shade under the oak tree.

My garden can literally run away from danger.

That is why I love containers. Especially grow bags.

Grow bags are light. They drain perfectly. They do not crack in the sun like plastic pots. And when you need to move a plant, you just grab the handles and go.

The Soursop I Killed Twice

Let me tell you about the tree my father gave me.

When we moved to Central Florida, my dad drove up from Miami with a soursop tree as a housewarming gift. Soursop is special. The fruit is sweet and creamy, makes the best juice, reminds you of home. He handed it to me with a nod. That is it. No instructions. No care tips. He is a man of few words.

So we planted it in the backyard. Same spot where we thought it would be happy. Good sun. Plenty of space.

That winter, the temperature dropped to 31 degrees.

The soursop died.

We did not tell him. We just went and bought another one. Put it in the same spot. Thought maybe the first one was just weak. We could take care of this one.

Winter came again. Another cold snap.

It died again.

Now I had killed my father's housewarming gift twice.

That is when I finally did some research. Turns out, soursop is a Zone 10b-11 plant. We are in Zone 10a. It can handle the heat. It loves the humidity. But one night below 35 degrees? Dead.

The solution was not better soil. It was not more water. It was not a different spot in the yard.

The solution was a pot.

The third soursop went into a 15-gallon grow bag. I keep it on the south side of the house where the brick wall radiates heat all day and into the night. When the weather report says frost is coming, I move it to the garage for thc night.

That tree is still alive. It is thriving. And my dad does not know I killed the first two. Well not until he reads this book.

The lesson

Some plants do not belong in the ground in your zone. But they can still belong in your garden if you give them wheels.

But Not Everything Belongs in a Pot

Now, before you think containers are the answer to everything, let me be honest.

I still manage to kill tomatoes in pots.

Even after everything I have learned about soil, water, and sun. Even after reading the tomato chapter in every gardening book. I put a tomato in a container, and somehow, it dies.

Too much water. Not enough water. Root-bound. Blossom end rot. Hornworms. Something always goes wrong.

So I gave up on container tomatoes. If I want tomatoes, I plant them in a raised bed in the fall and hope for the best.

The point is this: Containers are not magic. They are a tool. And like any tool, they work better for some jobs than others.

What Does Not Work in Containers

Deep-rooted plants: Cassava needs to go 3-4 feet deep. Sugarcane sends roots down just as far. You can grow them in a very large container (25+ gallons), but they will never reach their full size or production. If you want a real harvest, plant them in the ground.

Spreading plants: Pigeon peas want to sprawl. Bananas send up pups everywhere and create a whole clump. You can contain them, but you are fighting their nature. Let them spread in the ground and they will feed you for years.

Mature fruit trees: A mango tree can live in a pot for a few years while it is young. But once it starts fruiting, it needs room. The roots need space. The canopy needs space. You will get a few mangoes from a potted tree, but a tree in the ground will give you hundreds.

Start with 3-5 Plants, Not 50

Here is what nobody tells you when you see a list of "50+ plants you can grow in Florida":

Fifty plants is a lot.

It is a lot of watering. A lot of harvesting. A lot of pruning. A lot of managing.

If you try to plant all 50 at once, you will get overwhelmed. You will miss a watering day. A plant will die. Then another. Then you will feel like you failed and you will quit.

I have seen it happen over and over.

So here is my advice: Start with 3 to 5 plants.

Pick the ones your family will actually eat. Master those. Learn their rhythms. Figure out what they need and when they need it.

Then add more.

Microclimates: The Free Real Estate You Already Have

Now let's talk about something most gardening books skip over: **microclimates**[9].

A microclimate is a spot in your yard that has its own weather.

It might be 5 degrees cooler than the rest of the yard because it is shaded in the afternoon. It might stay 5 degrees warmer because it is next to a brick wall that radiates heat. It might be protected from wind. It might get frost when the rest of the yard does not.

Your yard is not one uniform zone. It is a collection of microclimates. And if you learn to see them, you can grow plants that technically should not survive in your area.

The Oak Tree I Hated

When we moved in, there was a massive oak tree in the backyard. I hated it.

It dropped leaves constantly. It shaded half the yard. It was in the way of where I wanted to plant.

I wanted it gone.

---

[9] A **microclimate** is a small, specific area within your yard where the temperature, light, or moisture levels differ from the rest of your property.

But we also had a coconut tree. And coconut trees do not really belong in Central Florida. We are too far north. Too cold in the winter. They survive, but they struggle.

Except ours was not struggling. It was thriving.

I could not figure out why until I stood outside one afternoon and really looked.

The oak tree was protecting the coconut.

The oak blocked the worst of the afternoon sun in the summer, so the coconut did not get scorched. It blocked the north wind in the winter, so the coconut did not get frost-burned. The oak created a microclimate under its canopy where the coconut could survive and thrive.

I stopped wanting to cut it down.

Now I plant shade-tolerant crops under that oak. Ginger. Turmeric. Taro. Things that want dappled light and protection from the brutal Florida sun.

That "unwanted" tree became one of the most valuable spots in my yard.

The Brick Wall

We have a brick wall on the south side of the yard. In the summer, that wall radiates heat. It turns the area in front of it into an oven.

Most plants would hate it. But pineapples? They love it.

Pineapples want heat. They want sun. They want to bake. So I plant all my pineapples along that wall. I also plant Barbados cherries there, which tolerate the heat and actually fruit better when they are hot.

That brick wall is a microclimate. And instead of fighting it, I use it.

The South Wall of the House

This is where my tender tropicals live when winter comes.

The south side of the house gets full sun all day. The wall absorbs heat during the day and radiates it at night. The roof overhang blocks frost. The house itself blocks the north wind.

On a night when the rest of the yard drops to 35 degrees, the south wall might stay at 40 or 42. That 5-degree difference is the difference between a plant surviving and a plant dying.

That is where the soursop goes when frost threatens. That is where I cluster my potted bananas, lemongrass, and anything else that cannot handle a freeze.

It is a microclimate. And it has saved more plants than I can count.

How to Find Your Microclimates

You do not need fancy equipment. You just need to pay attention.

Step 1: Stand outside for a few minutes at different times of day.

Where does the sun hit in the morning? Where does it linger in the afternoon? Where is it blocked by a tree, a fence, or the house?

Step 2: Notice the wind.

Where does it blow hardest? Where is it calm? Is there a corner of the yard that is always still, even when the rest of the yard is whipping around?

Step 3: Check for frost.

On a cold morning, walk your yard. Where is the frost thickest? Where is there no frost at all? Those frost-free spots are your warm microclimates.

Step 4: Feel the ground.

In the afternoon, put your hand on the soil in different parts of the yard. Where is it coolest? Where is it hottest? Soil temperature matters just as much as air temperature.

Once you know your microclimates, you can start matching plants to them.

Heat-lovers go by the brick wall. Shade-tolerant crops go under the oak. Tender tropicals go by the south wall. Cold-hardy plants go in the open yard where they can handle frost.

You are not fighting your yard. You are working with it.

Containers, Raised Beds, or Ground?

People always ask, "Which is better: containers, raised beds, or planting in the ground?"

The answer is: **All three.**

I use all three. They each have a job.

Containers = Flexibility and Survival

Containers are for plants that need to move. Tender tropicals. Experiments. Anything you might want to bring inside or shift to a different microclimate.

They are also for small spaces. If you only have a patio or a balcony, containers are your garden.

The only mistake people make is choosing pots that are too small. A plant cannot grow roots where there is no room. If you want a plant to thrive, give it a container it can stretch in.

A 5-gallon pot is the minimum for most vegetables and small fruiting plants. A 15-gallon pot is better. For dwarf fruit trees, go 20-25 gallons.

Raised Beds = Control

Raised beds are for vegetables. Greens. Herbs. Anything you want close to the kitchen door where you can grab it for dinner.

You choose the soil. You choose the drainage. You create the world the plant lives in.

But raised beds dry out faster than the ground. They need mulch. They need consistent watering. They are like children. If you show up for them, they flourish.

Ground = The Long Game

The ground is for permanence. Fruit trees. Banana clumps. Sugarcane. Pigeon peas. Cassava. Anything built to stay.

When a plant can root deep, it becomes strong. It can handle drought. It can handle wind. It anchors itself and does not need you to baby it.

But Florida soil can be stubborn. Sandy. Hungry. So you feed it with compost and mulch and time. And once the ground becomes alive, it will give back for years.

The Real Question

The real question is not "Where should I plant?"

The real question is: What can your life hold right now?

If you are overwhelmed, start small. Three plants. Maybe five.

If you are working full time, choose crops that do not need babysitting. Mulberries. Loquats. Moringa.

Your garden should not drain you. Your garden should meet you where you are.

You are growing a lifestyle. Not a photo.

Let me say it plain: Stop trying to prove you are a gardener. Just grow food.

Garden Reflection

Go outside. Look at your space. Do not judge it. Do not wish it was bigger or prettier.

Ask yourself: Where does joy live in this space?

By the door. By the window. By the fence. By the kitchen. Under the tree.

Whatever spot feels like life, that is where your first plant goes.

Write it down. That is your starting point.

Chapter 4: Pests, Diseases & Garden Resilience

The Hidden Enemies Nobody Warns You About

If soil, sun, and water are the basics, pests and diseases are the reality check. Every gardener, especially in Florida, will face them. You cannot avoid it, but you can prepare for it.

When I started, I thought every bug was an enemy. If it crawled, I squashed it. If leaves looked spotted, I panicked. Half the time, I was stressing over nothing, or worse, making the problem bigger.

But here is what nobody tells you about Florida pests and diseases:

The ones you can see are not the ones that will destroy you.

Everyone Talks About Aphids and Hornworms

Go to any gardening forum, read any Florida gardening book, and they will tell you about aphids and hornworms.

Aphids cluster on new growth and suck the life out of your plants. Hornworms are fat green caterpillars that can strip a tomato plant bare in two days.

Yes, those are real problems. I have dealt with both.

But you can SEE aphids. You can SEE hornworms. And when you can see the enemy, you can fight it.

The enemies that will actually ruin your garden? You cannot see them until it is too late.

Nematodes: The Underground Assassins

Let me tell you about the lemon tree I kept for four years.

I planted it with hope. It was going to give us fresh lemonade, key lime pie vibes, something special.

The first year, it grew a little. Put out some leaves. I was proud.

The second year, it just sat there. Green. Alive. But not growing.

I thought maybe it needed time to establish. Maybe the roots were spreading underground where I could not see them. So I waited.

Year three. Still sitting there. Same size. Same green leaves. No new growth.

I fertilized it. I amended the soil around it. I watered it carefully. I moved it to a sunnier spot.

Still nothing.

Year four. My husband got fed up.

One day while I was at work, he dug it up.

I came home and saw the hole where my lemon tree used to be, and I was furious. How dare he kill my tree? I was still holding out hope. It was still green. It could still come back.

He showed me the root ball.

There were barely any roots left. What was there was covered in knobby, swollen galls. The roots looked like they had tumors.

Nematodes.

The tree was not "establishing." It was dying a slow death underground while I kept watering it and hoping.

I had wasted four years on a tree that was already dead.

What Are Nematodes and Why Does Nobody Warn You?

Nematodes are microscopic worms that live in the soil. You cannot see them. You cannot spray them. You cannot pick them off.

They burrow into plant roots and feed on them from the inside. As they feed, they cause the roots to swell into galls (those knobby bumps I saw on my lemon tree). The plant cannot absorb water or nutrients through damaged roots, so it starves.

Above ground, the plant looks okay. Maybe a little stunted. Maybe the leaves are a little yellow. But nothing dramatic. Nothing that screams "emergency."

So you keep watering. You keep fertilizing. You keep waiting for it to grow.

And underground, the nematodes keep eating.

By the time you figure out what is happening, the plant is already too far gone.

What I Lost to Nematodes

Peppers. I planted a row of sweet peppers one spring. They grew for a few weeks, then just stopped. Leaves stayed green, but no new growth. No flowers. No fruit. I pulled one up to check the roots. Barely anything there. Just galls.

Sweet potatoes. This one hurt the most. Sweet potatoes take 3-4 months to grow. You plant the slips, you wait, you watch the vines spread. Everything looks healthy above ground.

Then you dig them up at harvest, excited to see what you grew.

And the potatoes are full of holes. Pitted. Scarred. Ruined.

All that time. All that waiting. And the nematodes destroyed them underground where I could not see.

How to Know If You Have Nematodes

Pull up a plant that is not growing right. Look at the roots.

Healthy roots are white or light tan, smooth, and spread out like fingers.

Nematode-damaged roots are brown, stunted, and covered in swollen galls that look like little knots or tumors.

If you see galls, you have nematodes.

What I Do Now

I cannot kill nematodes. Once they are in the soil, they are there.

But I can manage them.

Marigolds. I plant marigolds around my vegetable beds. Marigolds release a chemical from their roots that repels some species of nematodes. It is not a cure, but it helps.

Crop rotation. I do not plant the same thing in the same spot year after year. Nematodes target specific plant families. If you keep planting tomatoes in the same bed, the nematode population builds up. Rotate to something they do not like (like corn or beans), and the population drops.

Solarization. In the summer, I cover problem beds with clear plastic and let the sun cook the soil for 4-6 weeks. The heat kills nematodes, weed seeds, and fungal spores. It is brutal and effective.

Containers. For plants that nematodes love (peppers, tomatoes, okra), I plant them in containers with fresh, nematode-free soil. Problem solved.

Slugs: The Post-Rain Plague

Here is another enemy nobody warns you about.

You get a good rain. A real soaker. Two inches in an afternoon.

You are so happy. Free water! No need to drag the hose out for a few days!

So you skip watering. You give your garden a break. You give yourself a break.

Two days later, you walk outside to check on things.

And your seedlings are gone.

Not wilted. Not drooping. Gone. Stems chewed down to nubs. Leaves reduced to lace.

You look closer and see them: **slugs**.

Fat, slimy, slow-moving destroyers hiding under leaves and in the mulch. Their shells look innocent. Harmless. Decorative, even.

But in two days, they can wipe out an entire row of seedlings.

What I Do Now

Diatomaceous earth. After every heavy rain, I sprinkle diatomaceous earth around my vulnerable plants. It is a white powder made from crushed fossils. It is harmless to people and pets, but it shreds slugs when they crawl over it.

The problem is rain washes it away. So after every rain, I reapply. It is annoying. But it works.

Hand-picking. I go out in the evening or early morning when slugs are active, and I pick them off. I drop them in a bucket of soapy water.

Some people can just grab them. I cannot. They are slimy and gross.

So I cut the leaf they are on and toss the whole thing. Same with hornworms. People say, "Just pick them off." Have you seen a hornworm? They are huge. They are bright green and fat and horrifying.

I am not touching that. I cut the entire leaf and throw it in the trash.

Practical beats perfect every time.

Diseases: Florida Humidity Is on Team Fungus

Unlike pests, diseases do not crawl across your leaves. They creep in slow. Yellowing. Spots. Mildew. Sudden wilting. Florida humidity makes it worse because everything damp wants to grow fungus.

I once lost an entire grove of young mangoes to anthracnose, a nasty fungal disease that loves our wet, stagnant air. One week they looked green and healthy. The next week, the leaves were covered in black, sunken spots and the new fruit began to shrivel and drop.

I tried cutting infected leaves. I tried spraying. I tried babying them back to health. But once fungus takes hold in our climate, you are fighting an uphill battle.

Why Mangoes Are Different

When you grow squash, you're dealing with a season. When you lose a mango tree to disease, you're losing years of work. Mangoes are prone to anthracnose [10] and powdery mildew because they have thick canopies that hold onto moisture. If you don't keep that airflow moving, you're just building a greenhouse for mold.

The Trick Is Prevention

Florida humidity is already on team fungus. Do not make it easier.

Do not jam plants too close together. If air cannot move between them, you are building a disease hotel.

Do not water the leaves. Water the roots. Morning is best, so leaves dry before nightfall. Evening watering just leaves everything damp all night, and that is an invitation for mildew and fungal rot.

Mulch the soil. Rain splashes soil onto leaves, and soil carries fungal spores. A thick layer of mulch stops the splash.

Pull sick plants fast. Do not baby a plant that is clearly done. Pull it. Toss it in the trash (not the compost). Move on.

---

[10] Think of anthracnose as the "rot" that hits when your tree can't breathe. It isn't just about bad luck; it's a signal that your tree's canopy is too thick and holding too much moisture, creating the perfect environment for fungus to take hold.

A diseased plant left standing is just a buffet for problems. It spreads to the plants next to it. Then those spread it further.

Cut your losses. Replant fresh.

The Helpers You Did Not Ask For

Now let's talk about the creatures that are actually helping, even if you did not invite them.

Frogs. Frogs will chow down on mosquitoes, beetles, and slugs all night long. Do I scream when one jumps out of the mulch while I am weeding? Absolutely. Do I mess with them? Nope. I respect the job they are doing.

Lizards. In Florida, lizards are everywhere. They sunbathe on your fence, zip across your yard, and snack on the bugs you do not want. You do not have to love them. But let them work. Think of them as unpaid employees you did not hire but desperately need.

Ladybugs and lacewings. These eat aphids. A single ladybug can eat 50 aphids a day. If you spray broad-spectrum chemicals to kill aphids, you also kill the ladybugs. Then the aphids come back with no natural predators, and you are stuck spraying forever.

Let the good bugs do their job.

I Stopped Expecting Perfection

Here is the truth nobody tells you:

Grocery store produce looks flawless because it is sprayed, waxed, and polished. It is grown in monoculture fields with industrial pest control.

Backyard produce? It might have a scar. A bug bite. A funky shape.

But it is real. It is fresh. And it is yours.

I used to stress over every imperfection. Every chewed leaf. Every blemish.

Now I know: a few bites are part of real gardening.

If the pests are taking over, the plant is probably already stressed. Fix the soil. Fix the water. Fix the sun. A healthy plant can handle a few bugs.

But if a plant is clearly done? Pull it. Do not waste time trying to save something that wants to die.

Your garden is not a museum. It is a living, messy, resilient ecosystem.

Let it be imperfect.

Garden Reflection

Go outside and find one plant that does not look perfect.

Do not fix it. Do not judge it. Do not compare it to a picture in your mind.

Just notice it.

Then write: What is this plant teaching me about patience, power, or letting go?

Even one sentence is enough.

The Toni Pledge

Repeat after me:

I pledge not to panic at every bug.

I pledge to pull what is done and replant fresh.

I pledge to let frogs, lizards, and ladybugs work for me.

Chapter 5: Now You're Ready

Time to Grow What Actually Works

By now you have heard me rant about soil, sun, water, pests, and mindset.

If you are still here, you are already ahead of where I started. Because I did not listen to any of this in the beginning. I just went out, bought whatever looked cute at the garden store, and prayed it would grow.

Spoiler: it did not.

But here is the good news.

Once you understand the basics, gardening gets a whole lot less frustrating and a whole lot more rewarding.

You Cannot Outsmart Florida

At some point, you realize the truth: **You cannot outsmart Florida.** The sun is hotter than you. The bugs are faster than you. The rain will not ask your permission. The cold snaps show up unannounced, and the hurricanes do not care about your planting schedule.

The sooner you stop fighting all of that and start rolling with it, the easier this gets.

You stop wasting years of your life babying a peach tree that isn't meant for your chill hours, or a mango that can't handle the local humidity, just because the garden store made it look pretty on a flyer. You stop trying to force a "northern" orchard dream into a tropical, sandy reality.

Instead, you start building a food forest that actually feeds you and your family—on Florida's terms, not yours.

Florida Will Still Test You

Do not misunderstand me. Gardening in Florida is still hard.

The heat will cook plants alive. The storms will knock them flat. The bugs will show up uninvited. The nematodes will destroy things underground where you cannot see them. The slugs will eat your seedlings the moment you stop watching.

But now? You will not panic.

You will adjust. You will recover. And you will keep growing.

Because now you know:

Bad soil when you see it, and how to fix it. You are not trying to garden in beach sand anymore. You are building living soil.

How to read your yard's sunlight like a map. You know where the heat lives. You know where the shade saves lives. You know your microclimates.

How to water smarter, not harder. Deep watering. Morning watering. Let the roots chase the moisture instead of drowning them daily.

When to let the helpers do their job. Frogs, lizards, ladybugs. They are working for you even when you are not watching.

What to grow and what to skip. Not everything belongs in your garden just because it is pretty or popular. You grow food your family actually eats.

A Few Reminders Before You Start Planting

Ground is for permanence. Fruit trees. Bananas. Sugarcane. Cassava. Anything built to stay, belongs in the earth.

Raised beds give you control. You choose the soil. You choose what grows.

Containers give you flexibility. Move them when the weather turns. Protect tender plants. Experiment without commitment.

Size matters. The smaller the container, the more often you water and the less your plant produces. Do not cheap out on pot size.

Budget wisely. A $5 bag of soil in a $2 bucket can grow more food than a $200 raised bed left empty. Start small and scale up.

Experiment first. If you are not sure a crop belongs in your yard, try it in a container before committing to the ground.

What This Garden Is Really About

A garden is not about impressing strangers online.

It is not about having the biggest tomato or the most Instagram-worthy harvest basket.

It is about walking outside, picking fresh food, and putting it on your table.

For me, that means mangoes, bananas, guavas, greens my kids will eat, and herbs that end up in dinner almost every night.

For you, it might look different. And that is the beauty of it.

Your garden does not have to look like mine. It does not have to look like the picture in the book or the setup you saw on YouTube.

It just has to work for you.

The Plants That Earned Their Spot

So now that you have got the foundation, let's get into the plants.

These fifty-plus plants are not just random picks. They are the ones that earned their spot in my Florida garden.

Some are easy wins. Plant them, water them, walk away, and they will still produce.

Some are stubborn. They will test you. But once you figure them out, they will reward you for years.

And some will blow your mind once you understand how they grow. Things you thought were exotic or impossible? They thrive here. They want to grow here. You just have to give them the right conditions.

Every plant in the next section earned its spot because I lived through the wins and the fails with it.

I am giving you the shortcuts I wish I had before wasting time and money.

That way you can skip the headache and get straight to the harvest.

One Last Thing

Grab your gloves.

Or do not. Half the time I am out there with bare hands anyway.

Just get started.

Because the best garden is not the one you plan perfectly.

It is the one you actually plant.

The Toni Pledge

Repeat after me:

I pledge to keep it simple.

I pledge to start with one plant I actually want to eat.

I pledge to keep going, even if something flops.

Now let's grow some food.

Top 50+ Plants Made for the Heat

Figure 4 Our Backyard today

1. Sugarcane

Florida's Sweet Secret That Grows Like Crazy

Let me tell you about sugarcane.

In Miami, you could buy it on the street. Vendors would sell it in long sticks, already cut, ready to chew. We would grab one and walk home gnawing on it like natural candy, juice running down our chins, not caring that we looked ridiculous. It was sweet. It was refreshing. It kept you cool in the heat.

My cousins and I would have contests to see who could chew the longest piece. We would sit on the porch with sticky hands and purple-stained shirts, spitting out the pulp like we were professional sugarcane eaters.

That was childhood.

Now? You can barely find sugarcane in stores. And when you do, it is expensive and half-dried out.

But I can walk outside and cut my own.

Sugarcane grows in Florida like it was born here. Fast. Thick. Almost like bamboo. It loves the heat. It loves the sun. It does not ask for much, and it gives you that same sweetness I remember from those Miami streets.

If you want to feel like you are 10 years old again, plant sugarcane.

1. Sugarcane

How to Plant It

Here is the thing about sugarcane: you do not plant it from seeds. You plant it from a piece of cane.

That is right. You take a cutting from an existing stalk, and that cutting becomes your new plant. Once you grow it once, you never need to buy more. You just keep replanting pieces from your own harvest.

Step 1: Get a Cutting

You need a piece of stalk with at least one or two nodes. Nodes are the bumps or joints on the cane where new growth will pop out. Think of them like the knuckles on your finger. That is where the magic happens.

Step 2: Dig a Shallow Trench

Find a spot in full sun. Sugarcane wants all the sun you can give it. Dig a trench that is wide and shallow, about two inches deep.

Step 3: Lay It Sideways

This is not like planting a tree where you stick it upright. You lay the cutting sideways in the trench. You want the whole thing touching the soil.

Step 4: Cover Lightly and Keep It Moist

Cover the cutting with soil. Not buried deep. Just lightly covered. Water it. Keep it moist for the first few weeks.

Shoots will start popping up from those nodes within 2-3 weeks. By month two, you will have multiple stalks growing from that one piece you planted.

It is wild to watch.

Where and How It Thrives

Sugarcane needs space. Not a little corner by the fence. Real space.

It gets tall. Six to ten feet, sometimes more. It gets thick. The stalks grow in clumps, spreading out as they mature.

Can you grow it in a container?

Technically, yes. But you need a very large pot. Think 25 gallons or bigger. And even then, it will not reach its full size or produce as much as it would in the ground.

If you have the yard space, plant it in the ground. Let it spread. Let it become a privacy wall. Because that is what happens when you plant a row of sugarcane. It grows so thick and tall that it blocks the view, blocks the wind, and turns into a living fence.

Best Time to Plant: February through August. It loves warm soil and sun. Do not plant it in the winter. It will just sit there waiting for warmth.

How to Care for It

Sugarcane is not picky, but it is a heavy feeder.

Soil: It loves rich, well-draining soil with high organic matter. If your soil is sandy (and let's be honest, in Florida it probably is), mix in compost or aged manure before planting.

Fertilizer: A balanced fertilizer every 6-8 weeks during the growing season keeps it happy. Or use compost tea if you are going the organic route.

Mulch: Mulch around the base to lock in moisture and keep weeds down. Sugarcane does not like competition.

Water: Keep it consistently moist, especially in the first few months. Once it is established, it can handle some drought, but it produces sweeter stalks when it gets regular water.

Pests & Disease Prevention

Sugarcane is pretty tough, but it has two main enemies:

Aphids and Mealybugs

These little pests love to cluster on the stalks and suck the sap. If you see them, blast them off with a strong spray of water. If they come back, hit them with neem oil [11]early before they multiply and invite sooty mold.

Orange Rust

If you see reddish powdery spots on the leaves, that is orange rust. It is a fungal disease. Remove those leaves right away and improve air circulation by thinning out crowded stalks.

The best prevention? Do not plant sugarcane in the same spot year after year. Rotate where you plant it every few years to keep soil-borne pests and diseases from building up.

Time to Harvest

About 9 to 12 months after planting, your sugarcane is ready.

How do you know?

The stalks get thick. The bottoms start turning from green to tan or light brown. The cane feels solid when you squeeze it.

Cut the stalks at the base with a sharp machete or garden saw. Do not pull them. Cut them clean.

And here is the beauty: **the roots stay in the ground and send up new shoots.** So you get a second harvest without replanting. Sometimes a third. You are basically growing a perennial candy factory.

What It Tastes Like (For Real)

Sweet. Earthy. Like grass, but in the best way.

---

[11] **Neem oil** is a natural, organic pesticide and fungicide extracted from the seeds of the neem tree, a tropical evergreen native to India.

You chew it like a snack. You do not eat the pulp. You just chew, suck out the juice, and spit out the fiber.

It is juicy. It is refreshing. And it brings you right back to being a kid with sticky hands and no worries.

What No One Tells You

It grows FAST. Like bamboo-level fast. In the right conditions, you can see new growth every week.

Once you grow it, you never need to buy more. Every time you harvest, you replant a piece. It is self-sustaining.

It makes an incredible privacy wall. Plant a row of it, and within a year, you have a living fence that is thick, tall, and tropical-looking.

Kids love it. Hand a child a piece of sugarcane and watch them figure it out. They will chew on it for an hour.

Kitchen Tip

Fresh Sugarcane Juice:

Chop the stalks into short pieces. Blend them with a splash of water. Strain through cheesecloth or a fine mesh strainer. Chill it with lime or ginger.

That is it. Fresh, natural, sweet juice with no added sugar.

Homemade Cane Syrup:

Take that juice and simmer it slowly on the stove until it reduces and thickens. You just made your own cane syrup. Pour it over pancakes, stir it into tea, drizzle it on fruit.

Toni's Tip

Freeze bite-sized pieces of sugarcane and toss them into iced tea or lemonade. They act like flavor-infusing ice cubes. It is a backyard treat that brings me right back to childhood every single time.

1. Sugarcane

Did You Know?

Sugarcane is the number one crop grown in Florida by dollar value. More than oranges. More than strawberries. More than anything else.

Commercial growers have acres and acres of it. But you do not need acres.

You just need a sunny spot and a willingness to let it take over.

And here is something wild: Raw sugarcane has been used for generations as a natural toothbrush.

Chewing on fresh stalks stimulates saliva production, which helps clean your gums and neutralize bacteria. It gently scrubs your teeth while releasing trace minerals and nutrients that support oral health.

Just rinse your mouth afterward. Leftover juice can attract plaque if you do not clean up.

So yeah. Sugarcane is not just candy. It is also dental care. Nature is wild.

Why Sugarcane Earns Its Keep

I know, I know—everyone looks at sugarcane and just sees a giant stalk of pure sugar. But in my house, we look at it as a powerhouse. If you are going to spend the time and space to grow it, it might as well work for you.

When the kids have been running hard in the yard and need a pick-me-up, a quick press of fresh cane juice is a clean, natural boost. It's a sugar rush that doesn't come with the dreaded crash of a candy bar or a soda. On those brutal Florida afternoons when the humidity is pulling the life right out of you, it's incredibly hydrating, acting almost like a natural electrolyte drink that actually replenishes you rather than just masking the thirst.

Beyond the energy, you are getting something truly functional. It is packed with antioxidants that help fight off the daily stress of living in this heat, and it has a long, storied history of supporting kidney health and keeping digestion smooth—which, let's be honest, is a benefit every parent can appreciate. When you drink it raw and fresh, you aren't just getting sugar; you arc getting all the minerals and life-force that the plant pulled directly from your soil. Treat it like a luxury, not a soda, and it will be one of the best things you ever grow.

Best for: Full sun, in-ground planting, kids who need a natural distraction, anyone who wants a privacy wall that is also edible.

1. Sugarcane

Figure 5 Our Sugarcane Patch used as a Privacy Fence

2. Watermelon

The Backyard Snack That Beats the Heat

We keep growing watermelons, not just because they thrive in this Florida heat, but because they hold a piece of our heart.

This was the very first plant I ever grew, right before I had my daughter. Maybe that is why it is her favorite to this day.

Florida heat will have you out here feeling like you are on the surface of the sun. And when that wave hits? Ain't nothing like cutting into your own homegrown watermelon. That first bite? Yes.

But there is more to it than just cooling off.

My father-in-law was probably the proudest of our watermelons. Every summer, he would light up and say, "Toni, I can't wait to try those watermelons." That pushed me to grow them bigger, better, and with even more love.

We lost him this year, right before the melons came in. He did not get to see them ripen, but I know he is still smiling down. Every time I see one growing, I hear his voice and feel his pride.

That is why we keep growing them. For the heat. For the kids. For the memories. For him.

2. Watermelon

Best Planting Time

Start your planting anytime between March and July. Watermelons do not just like the heat; they crave it. They need those long, sweltering days and warm nights to pack the sugar into the fruit. If you are planting in the heat of July, just be ready to keep them hydrated.

Skip the overpriced nursery seedlings and stick with seeds. They are cheap, and there is something magical about watching your kids plant them and seeing them take off in just a few days. Whatever you do, never plant these flat on the ground. Pile up a little mound of soil about six inches high to get the roots up and out of the swamp. Florida soil stays wet too long after a heavy rain, and soggy roots are a death sentence for a watermelon.

Drop two or three seeds in each mound, and once they sprout, be ruthless: pull out the weaker ones and let the strongest plant own the space. Give them at least three to four feet of room between those mounds. These vines are natural runners, and if you crowd them, you are just asking for mildew and stunted fruit. Forget the chemical bloom boosters, too. Before you plant, mix a generous helping of finished compost or worm castings into the mound. That is the secret to a melon that is actually sweet instead of bland and watery.

Pro-Tip from the Garden: When you see a melon starting to form, slide a piece of cardboard or a dry shingle underneath it. It keeps the fruit off the damp soil, which prevents rot and keeps the bugs from snacking on your harvest before you do.

Can It Grow in a Pot?

Yes, but you need a large container. Think 20-30 gallons minimum.

Let the vines spill over the sides. Support the fruit with a sling or prop it up so it does not sit in soggy soil and rot.

If you are tight on space, grow a mini variety like Sugar Baby or Bush Sugar Baby. They are bred for containers and still give you that sweet, juicy fruit.

How to Care for It

Sun: Full sun. 6 to 8 hours or more. Watermelons are sun worshippers.

Water: Deep water 2-3 times a week. Once the fruit starts forming, back off a little. Overwatering at that stage waters down the sweetness.

Soil: Loose, well-draining, and nutrient-rich. Sandy loam with a slightly acidic pH (6.0-6.8) is best. Work in compost before planting to improve moisture retention.

Pollination Tip: Bees help a lot. But if you are short on pollinators, you can do it yourself. Gently move pollen from the male flowers (the ones on long stems with no fruit behind them) to the female flowers (the ones with a tiny melon already forming at the base) using a small brush or even your finger.

Pest & Disease Prevention

When it comes to pests and disease, you have to be one step ahead of the garden. Watermelons are magnets for aphids, cucumber beetles, and those dreaded squash vine borers, but you don't need to reach for a chemical sprayer the moment you see a bug.

Start by using lightweight row covers when your seedlings are young. It acts like a protective tent, keeping the pests away while the plant is vulnerable. Just make sure you pull those covers off the second you see flowers, because those pollinators need to get in there to do their job.

After that, the best thing you can do is rotate your planting spots every single year. If you plant in the exact same dirt over and over, you are just inviting soil-borne diseases like fusarium wilt to set up shop and take down your whole crop.

Finally, stay disciplined with your water. Always aim for the base of the plant in the early morning. If you are splashing water onto the leaves in the evening, you are creating a damp, dark environment that makes powdery mildew inevitable. Keep the leaves dry, keep the air moving, and you'll spend a lot less time fighting fires and a lot more time enjoying your harvest.

Time to Harvest

80-100 days after planting.

How to Know It Is Ready: The tendril near the fruit stem (see figure 6) is dry and brown. This is the most reliable sign.

2. Watermelon

Figure 6 Tendril

The underside has a creamy yellow patch where the melon rested on the ground.

It sounds hollow when you knock on it. Give it a thump. If it sounds like a drum, it is ready.

Do not pick too early. A watermelon will not ripen off the vine. If you cut it too soon, it will be pale, crunchy, and disappointing.

Health Benefits

You don't need a medical degree to know that watermelon is the ultimate Florida survival food. When the humidity is sitting at 90 percent and the sun feels like it's right on top of you, this is the harvest you want waiting in the garden.

Beyond the fact that it is loaded with water, making it the most refreshing way to rehydrate after an afternoon working in the yard—you are getting a massive dose of Vitamin C and lycopene [12]in every bite. That is a direct win for your heart and your skin, which, let's be honest, takes a beating in this climate. It's naturally low in calories and helps keep digestion and inflammation in check, too.

When you grow these yourself, you aren't just getting a grocery store melon that's been sitting on a truck for a week. You're getting a fresh, nutrient-dense treat that tastes like sunshine. It's the perfect, guilt-free reward for the work you put in to keep your garden running.

---

[12] Lycopene is the natural pigment that gives watermelon and tomatoes their vibrant red color, but it's much more than just a dye. Think of it as a heavy-duty antioxidant that helps your body fight off the cellular damage caused by our intense Florida sun. It's essentially a natural shield for your skin and heart, helping to keep you healthy while you're out there putting in the work in your garden.

2. Watermelon

What It Tastes Like (For Real)

Like summer exploded in your mouth.

Juicy, crisp, and so sweet it runs down your chin if you are not careful.

When you grow it yourself? It is like the watermelon remembered how to taste like watermelon again.

What No One Tells You

Do not overwater once the fruit starts forming. It will water down the sweetness. Let the plant dry out a little between waterings at that stage.

Try growing mini varieties if you do not have space. Sugar Baby and Bush Sugar Baby are perfect for small yards and containers.

Let the vines do their thing. They will look messy. They will sprawl everywhere. That is fine. The messier they look, the happier they usually are.

The rind is edible. Do not throw it away. Try pickling it. It is sweet, crunchy, and delicious.

Best Varieties for Florida Heat

Want watermelon that grows fast, survives the sun, and actually fits your space? Try one of these:

Sugar Baby – Small, sweet, and perfect for pots

Crimson Sweet – Classic flavor and heat-tolerant

Charleston Gray – Big, juicy, and Florida strong

Jubilee – Giant, super sweet, and a vine beast

Golden Midget – Turns yellow when ripe (yes, really)

Bush Sugar Baby – Same sweetness, bush-style for containers

Toni's Pick: I always go back to Sugar Baby. Fast, manageable, and easy to grow even in a raised bed.

2. Watermelon

Kitchen Tip

Chop it cold and eat it straight, or blend it with lime juice for a quick slush.

You can also freeze cubes for smoothies or mix it into a watermelon-mint salad with a pinch of sea salt.

Do not sleep on watermelon juice. Especially if you are pregnant, hot, or just over it. It is like a glass of instant refresh.

Toni's Tip

Let your kids drop a seed in the ground and watch it take off.

Watermelon is what pulled me into gardening in the first place. Now it is something we look forward to every summer.

Did You Know?

Watermelon is actually a cousin of cucumber and squash.

And Florida grows more watermelon than almost any other state in the U.S.

3. Peanuts

The Snack Treasure That Grows Itself Underground

My grandma was from Haiti, and I will never forget coming home from school to find her sitting on the porch, always snacking on peanuts. It was her thing. Simple, comforting, and somehow always waiting.

She passed at 86 years young, God bless her soul, but that memory stuck.

One day, I was at Publix and saw a giant bag of raw peanuts in that aisle when you're leaving produce, right before you turn and hit the fresh seafood. The price was good, and something clicked. "Can I grow this?"

I figured, why not try?

Turns out, peanuts love this Florida heat. And now every time we harvest them, I think of her. Sitting on that porch. Shelling peanuts with her hands. Content.

We call this "snack treasure" at my house. Because that is exactly what it feels like when you pull up a plant and find 30 to 50 peanuts hiding underground.

How to Grow It

When to plant: March through June. Peanuts need about 4 to 5 months of warm weather to grow and mature.

What you need: Raw peanuts. Not roasted. Roasted peanuts are dead. You are trying to plant life, not a snack. Grab raw peanuts from the store—the ones with the papery skin still on work best.

Shell them gently. Try not to rip that skin off. That skin protects the seed.

Dig a shallow hole, about 1 to 2 inches deep. Drop a peanut in. Cover it. Space them about 5 to 6 inches apart.

And here is the most important part: **keep the soil loose.** Do not pack it down. Do not walk on it. Peanuts grow underground, and if the soil is compacted like concrete, they cannot form properly. They need room to bury themselves.

In about 7 to 10 days, green leaves will pop up. You will feel like a genius.

A few weeks later, yellow flowers bloom. Pretty little things. And then those flowers do something wild: they dive into the soil to form the pods.

The first time I saw it happen, I thought something was wrong. I Googled it like five times. "Why are my peanut flowers dying and falling into the dirt?"

Turns out, that is exactly what they are supposed to do. The flower blooms, gets pollinated, then the stem grows down into the ground and becomes a peanut.

Nature is weird. But it works.

Can you grow it in a pot?

Yes. But the pot needs to be deep. At least 12 inches. And wide enough for the plant to spread out.

Use loose, sandy soil. Not that heavy potting mix you bought for your houseplants. Peanuts need room to bury their pegs. (Pegs are what the flower stems turn into when they grow down into the soil to form pods. I know. It sounds made up. But that is what they are called.)

If your pot is too shallow or the soil is too dense, the plant will grow, it will flower, but you will not get peanuts. The pegs will hit the bottom of the pot or get stuck in compacted soil and just give up.

So go big on the pot. Go loose on the soil. And do not overthink it.

Taking care of it:

Peanuts are not high-maintenance. But they do have a few non-negotiables.

3. Peanuts

Give them full sun. At least 6 hours daily. Peanuts are sun worshippers. Shade makes them weak and unproductive.

Water regularly, especially when the plant is flowering. That is when it needs consistent moisture. But once the pods start forming underground, back off a little. Too much water at that stage can cause the peanuts to rot. Let the soil dry out slightly between waterings.

Your soil needs to be loose, sandy, and slightly acidic. pH between 5.8 and 6.2 is ideal. Do not compact it. I cannot say this enough. Heavy soil restricts the pegs from reaching down to form peanuts. If your soil is clay or hard-packed, amend it with sand and compost before you even think about planting.

And here is the thing about fertilizer: keep it light. Peanuts are legumes, which means they pull nitrogen from the air and store it in their roots. So they do not need a lot of fertilizer. In fact, too much nitrogen encourages leafy growth instead of peanuts. Add compost at planting, then leave it alone. Let the plant do its thing.

The enemies:

Squirrels are your biggest problem. They will smell those peanuts forming underground and dig them up the moment you are not looking. It is infuriating.

Cover the bed with netting once the pods start forming. Or accept that you are growing peanuts for the neighborhood wildlife. Your choice.

Aphids and thrips love peanut plants. If you see them clustering on the leaves, hit them with neem oil or insecticidal soap early. Do not wait. They multiply fast.

Leaf spot disease is common in Florida because of the humidity. Water at soil level, not on the leaves. And rotate your crops every year. Do not plant peanuts in the same spot two years in a row. The disease builds up in the soil and will wreck your next crop.

When to harvest:

120 to 150 days after planting. That is about 4 to 5 months. Peanuts take their time.

The plant will turn yellow and start to flop over. That is your signal. It is not dying. It is telling you the peanuts are done.

Pull up one plant gently. Check the pods. If they are fully formed and tan-colored, you are good. If they are still white or soft, give them another week or two.

Dig around the base of the plant with your hands or a small trowel. Pull the whole plant up carefully. The peanuts will be clinging to the roots underground like little treasures.

Shake off the dirt. Lay the whole plant out in a warm, dry spot for a few days to air-dry. Once the shells are dry and brittle, you can shell them or roast them whole.

Do not skip the drying step. Wet peanuts will mold. And moldy peanuts are not just gross, they can make you sick.

What No One Tells You

Peanuts are not actually nuts. They are legumes. Related to beans and peas, not almonds or cashews.

They help improve your soil by adding nitrogen. Plant peanuts one season, then follow up with a heavy feeder like tomatoes or squash. Your soil will thank you.

They grow right where the flower dives into the ground. It is wild to watch. The flower blooms, then the stem (called a peg) grows down into the soil and forms the peanut pod underground.

You do not need much space to get a good harvest. A 4x4 bed can give you pounds of peanuts.

And homegrown peanuts taste different. Sweeter. Fresher. Like the peanut remembered what it was supposed to taste like.

Boil them and it is like biting into warm, salty butter. Roast them and the crunch is next-level.

In the Kitchen

This is a Florida and Southern classic: put raw peanuts in a big pot, cover them with salted water, bring it to a boil, then turn it down and simmer for 1 to 2 hours until they are soft.

You can add garlic, Cajun seasoning, or even a Scotch bonnet if you are feeling bold. My family likes them spicy.

Drain them and eat them warm. They are soft, salty, and addictive. You will eat way more than you think you will.

Want them roasted? Spread raw peanuts (shells and all) on a baking sheet. Roast at 350°F for 20 minutes. Shake the pan halfway through so they roast evenly. Let them cool, shell them, eat them. Fresh roasted peanuts taste nothing like the store-bought kind. They are sweeter, richer, and you will wonder why you ever bought them in a bag.

Toni's Tip

We call this "snack treasure" at my house. We let our kids pull them up. It is fun. It is hands-on. And it makes them curious about growing more.

There is something magical about digging in the dirt and finding food you did not know was there.

Did You Know?

A single peanut plant can grow 30 to 50 peanuts. And it all starts with a flower that plants itself. Yeah, it literally dives underground to make food.

Nature does not make sense sometimes. But it works.

4. Cassava

The Root That Fed Generations (and Still Does)

Cassava is a Haitian staple. You will always find it next to beans or used in place of rice, especially with the older generation. It is hearty, filling, and real food.

One day, I was leaving my dad's house and he casually strolls up from the back, holding a few cassava cuttings. Did not say much. Just handed them to me and in Creole gave a warning: *"Pa mete yo konsa nan tè a."* (Don't plant them just like this in the dirt.)

My dad is a man of few words, but when he speaks, I listen.

I followed his lead, prepped the soil right, and gave it a try. Now here I am, growing cassava just like he taught me, passing it down again.

How to Grow It

Plant cassava from March through July. Once it is warm, cassava takes off.

You need a cutting from a mature cassava plant, about 6 to 8 inches long. You cannot grow cassava from seeds. You grow it from cuttings. Just like sugarcane.

Let the cutting dry out for a day or two before planting. This helps prevent rot. If you stick a fresh, wet cutting straight into the soil, it might just sit there and rot instead of rooting.

When you are ready to plant, stick it at an angle into loose soil. Bury about half of it. Do not plant it straight up and down like a fence post. Angle it.

And here is the critical part: do not plant it upside down. The side with buds (the little eyes, like on a potato) should be facing up. If you plant it upside down, it will not grow. Or it will struggle. And my dad did not raise me to struggle with cassava.

4. Cassava

If you see green buds forming on the cutting before you plant it, even better. That is your sign it is ready to grow.

You can grow cassava in a pot, but you need a large, deep container. Think 25 to 30 gallons or more. Cassava roots grow thick and deep. If the pot is too small, the roots will hit the bottom, get cramped, and you will end up with tiny, sad cassava that is not worth the effort.

If you have the yard space, plant it in the ground. Let it stretch. Let it do what it was meant to do.

Cassava is low-maintenance. It is a survivor.

Give it full sun. Six to eight hours daily. It loves heat. It does not complain about Florida summers.

Water it moderately when it is young. But once it is established, cassava is drought-tolerant. It can handle dry spells better than most plants. In fact, overwatering is worse than underwatering. Cassava does not like wet feet.

Your soil needs to be loose and well-draining. Sandy loam with a slightly acidic to neutral pH (5.5 to 7.0) is ideal. Here is the wild part: cassava thrives in poor soil. You do not need to amend it heavily. In fact, too much rich soil or fertilizer just makes the plant grow big leafy tops with small roots. You want the opposite. You want those thick, starchy roots underground.

Avoid heavy clay soil that traps water. Cassava will rot.

Watch for spider mites, whiteflies, and mealybugs. They love cassava leaves. If you see them, hit them with neem oil or insecticidal soap.

Cassava mosaic disease is the big one to worry about. It is a virus spread by whiteflies. The leaves get yellow mottled patterns and the plant stops growing properly. There is no cure. If you see it, pull the plant and toss it. Do not compost it.

The best prevention is to plant healthy, disease-free cuttings and give your plants space so air can move between them. Mulching helps suppress weeds and keep moisture consistent without waterlogging the roots.

4. Cassava

Figure 7 My Husband Jermaine Harvesting Cassava

Eight to twelve months. Cassava takes its time. You plant it and you wait. You check on it. You let it grow. And eventually, the leaves start yellowing and dropping.

That is cassava's way of saying "I'm ready."

Dig it up carefully. Use a shovel or fork and work around the base of the plant. The roots are thick and deep, so do not just yank it out or you will break them.

And here is the beauty: if you are not ready to harvest all of it, you can leave some in the ground. Cassava stores well in-ground. Just dig up what you need and leave the rest until you are ready.

What No One Tells You

You need to cook cassava fully before eating. Raw cassava contains natural toxins (cyanogenic glycosides). Boiling or frying breaks them down. Do not eat it raw. Do not feed it to your kids raw. Just cook it.

It stores well in-ground. If you are not ready to use it, leave it. It will wait for you.

The plant itself is beautiful. Tall, leafy, almost tropical looking. It adds height and structure to your garden even before you harvest.

4. Cassava

Once you grow it once, you will never need to buy it again. Just cut a piece of the stem, let it dry, and replant it. It keeps going.

And the taste? Cassava is creamy and dense. Like a firmer potato with a hint of sweetness. Fried, boiled, or mashed, it soaks up flavor like a champ.

In the Kitchen

Boil cassava in salted water until it is fork-tender. Then you can mash it, fry it, or serve it alongside fish and pikliz.

In Haitian cooking, it is used in soups, stews, or just boiled and eaten plain with a little butter and salt.

I love it fried golden with epis and a squeeze of lime. Crispy on the outside, soft and creamy on the inside.

You can even make cassava flour if you are fancy. But honestly, I just eat it fried.

Toni's Tip

Cassava taught me patience. It takes months to grow. But when you dig it up, it is like unearthing a meal your ancestors would have eaten.

And when it comes from your dad's hands, you listen. You grow. And you pass it on.

Did You Know?

4. Cassava

Cassava is the third most important food source in the tropics after rice and corn. It feeds more than 500 million people around the world.

And in Haiti, it is not just food. It is culture. It is history. It is survival.

Best for: Full sun, sandy soil, anyone with patience, anyone who wants to grow food that connects them to their roots (literally and figuratively).

Figure 8 Our Newly planted Cassava

5. Muscadine Grapes

The Tough Lesson That Turned Into Sweet Reward

Whew. This was one of those tough lessons.

I grabbed grape vines from the store thinking, "Grapes? Sure, I'll take one." No labels, no clue. Just said grape, so I planted it.

Then someone told me, "You need two different types if they're not self-fertile."

And I was like... wait, what?

Then my mother-in-law came by and casually mentioned I needed a trellis.

A what?

Eventually I got it together and now we have got muscadines growing like they own the place.

5. Muscadine Grapes

Figure 9 Backyard Grapevine

How to Grow It

Okay, so first thing: buy self-fertile varieties. Ison, Carlos, Southern Home. Write that down. Because if you buy the wrong kind, you will need two plants for them to pollinate each other. And nobody tells you that until after you have already spent the money and planted one.

Plant them late winter to early spring. January to March is best. But this is Florida, so you can plant into summer if you keep them watered and do not let them fry.

When you plant, dig a hole twice as wide as the root ball. Not deeper. Wider. You want those roots to spread out, not down. Plant in full sun. Muscadines need every bit of sun they can get.

And space them far apart. Like 10 to 20 feet apart. I know that sounds ridiculous. But these vines spread. They take over. If you plant them close together thinking you will save space, you will regret it when they tangle into each other and you cannot tell where one ends and the other begins.

Now here is the thing my mother-in-law told me that I wish I had known from day one: **put up a trellis immediately.** Not next week. Not when the vine gets bigger. Now.

Because muscadines grow fast. And if you do not give them something to climb, they will sprawl across the ground, wrap around your fence, climb your trees, and generally act like they own your yard.

I waited. I thought I had time. I did not. I spent an entire Saturday untangling vines that had wrapped around themselves like Christmas lights. It was miserable. Do not be me. Put up the trellis first.

5. Muscadine Grapes

Once they are in the ground, muscadines are pretty low-maintenance.

They want full sun. All day if you can give it to them. The more sun, the sweeter the grapes.

Water them deeply once a week. Especially in summer. They can handle some drought once they are established, but if you want big, juicy grapes, keep them watered.

The soil needs to drain well. Muscadines hate wet feet. If your soil is heavy clay that holds water, plant them on a mound so the roots do not sit in soggy soil and rot.

Add compost when you plant, but do not go crazy with fertilizer. Too much nitrogen makes big leafy vines with no fruit. You want fruit, not a jungle.

And you have to prune them. Every late winter, when they are dormant, cut back the previous year's growth. If you skip this, the vines turn into a tangled mess and fruiting drops off. Pruning keeps them productive and keeps you sane.

The main enemies are birds and raccoons. They will eat your grapes the second they ripen. Put netting over the vines or accept that you are growing fruit for wildlife.

Japanese beetles love grape leaves. If you see them, pick them off by hand or use traps. Do not spray chemicals. Muscadines are naturally tough. They do not need it.

Prune for airflow to prevent black rot and powdery mildew. Florida humidity invites fungus, but if the vines have space to breathe, they can handle it.

It takes 2 to 3 years before you get a real harvest. I know. That is a long time. But once they start producing, they keep going for decades.

Muscadines ripen mid to late summer. They do not all ripen at once, so you will be picking every few days for several weeks. When they are soft, sweet, and pull off the vine easily, they are ready.

Do not wait for the whole cluster to ripen. It will not happen. Pick what is ready and come back tomorrow for more.

What No One Tells You

Muscadines are native to the South. They love Florida heat. Unlike other grapes that struggle in humidity, muscadines thrive here.

5. Muscadine Grapes

Some varieties need a buddy (a pollinator) to fruit. That is why I tell you to pick self-fertile varieties. It saves you the headache.

You do not need to spray them. They are tough against pests and diseases. They practically grow themselves once they are established.

You can use the leaves like grape leaves for cooking. Yes, really. Stuff them with rice and meat, or use them to wrap fish before grilling.

And the taste? If a grape and a plum had a baby, it would be a muscadine. Sweet, tangy, and thick-skinned. You either chew the skin or pop the inside out like candy. Wild, juicy, and full of flavor.

In the Kitchen

Muscadines make amazing jelly, juice, and wine. You can also freeze them whole and pop them in smoothies or eat them frozen like grape ice cubes.

I like simmering them into a quick syrup for pancakes. Or tossing them into a salad with feta and arugula. The sweet-tart flavor cuts through rich dishes perfectly.

Toni's Tip

Do not overthink it. If you are unsure, plant two. Label everything. And get that trellis before the vines start wrapping around your shoes.

I learned the hard way. You do not have to.

Did You Know?

Muscadines are one of the few grapes that thrive in hot, humid climates without major disease problems. They have been grown in the South for over 400 years.

And they are packed with antioxidants, especially in the skin. High in resveratrol, which is linked to longevity. Good source of fiber and vitamin C. They support heart and brain health.

So yeah. You are not just growing grapes. You are growing medicine.

6. Citrus

Figure 10 Key limes in Rolling Pot

The Tree That'll Fruit... If You Stop Babying It.

Listen.

We have got citrus trees in the yard that have been here five years. Five. And still no fruit.

Every spring, I watch them. Green leaves. Strong branches. They look healthy. They look productive. They look like they should be dropping lemons by the dozen.

Nothing.

We call them "ornamental plants" now. Pretty leaves, great shade, no lemons in sight. My husband walks past them and shakes his head. I do not even look anymore.

Meanwhile, on the patio, I have got citrus in pots. Less than a year old. Small. Manageable. And they are loaded.

Lemons hanging heavy on the branches. Limes so thick I have to prop up the stems so they do not break. I walk out in the morning and pick fresh fruit for my water, my tea, my cooking. Every single day.

Did I learn a lesson? Oh yes.

Citrus loves containers here in Florida. And I wasted five years staring at those in-ground trees waiting for them to do something they were never going to do.

Best Planting Time

February through May. Or fall if you are in South Florida.

But if you are planting in a pot, you can plant almost anytime. Just do not move it when it is flowering or it will drop all the blooms and you will be back to square one.

How to Plant It

If you are planting in the ground, dig a wide hole. Not deep. Wide. Mix in well-draining soil because citrus hates soggy roots. Place the rootball slightly above ground level. Do not bury the base of the trunk. That is how you end up with sad roots and no fruit. Ask me how I know.

If you are planting in a pot (which I highly recommend), use a 15 to 25 gallon container with drainage holes. Do not cheap out on the pot size. Citrus needs room to spread its roots.

Use loose, well-draining soil. Cactus mix or citrus-specific soil works great. Regular potting soil holds too much water and citrus will just sit there sulking.

Water deeply right after planting. Mulch lightly around the base, but do not pile it against the trunk. Citrus trunks need air or they rot.

Can It Grow in a Pot?

Yes. And in Florida, citrus actually does better in pots.

I know that sounds backwards. But in a pot, you control everything. You can move it during cold snaps. You can bring it closer to the house when a freeze is coming.

In the ground, you are at the mercy of Florida's unpredictable weather and whatever soil you have got. And if your soil is heavy clay, your citrus will struggle for years. Like mine did.

Pots give you control. And citrus in pots tends to fruit faster. Especially lemons and limes.

How to Care for It

Citrus wants full sun. Six to eight hours daily. The more sun, the more fruit.

Water it, but let the soil dry out slightly between waterings. Overwatering is the number one reason citrus does not fruit.

Feed it with a citrus-specific fertilizer every six weeks during the growing season (spring and summer). Do not use a high-nitrogen fertilizer. You want flowers, not just leaves.

If temps dip below 40°F, bring potted citrus near the house or wrap it with a blanket. Citrus can handle a light freeze, but anything prolonged will damage it.

Pests and Problems

Watch for citrus leaf miners. They tunnel through the leaves and leave squiggly trails. Prune infected leaves.

Scale insects and aphids love citrus. Encourage ladybugs and lacewings. They will eat the pests for you. If the infestation is bad, use neem oil or insecticidal soap.

The big one to worry about is citrus greening[13]. It is a disease spread by tiny insects called psyllids. Once a tree has it, there is no cure. The tree slowly declines and dies.

---

[13] Citrus greening, often called Huanglongbing (HLB) or "yellow dragon disease," is a devastating, incurable bacterial infection that acts like a clog in the tree's vascular system.
It is spread by a tiny, sap-sucking insect called the Asian citrus psyllid. Once the bacteria enter the tree, they block the flow of nutrients and sugars, essentially starving the tree from the inside out.

The best prevention is to buy trees from certified nurseries and watch for psyllids. If you see them, treat early.

When to Harvest

Lemons and limes take 6 to 9 months from flowering to harvest.

Oranges and grapefruits take 9 to 12 months.

You will know they are ready when they feel heavy in your hand. When you give them a gentle twist and they release from the branch without a fight. If you have to yank, they are not ready. Let them be.

Do not pick them early thinking they will ripen on the counter like a tomato. Citrus does not ripen after picking. What you pick is what you get.

What No One Tells You

Too much water equals no fruit. Citrus needs a little stress to produce. If you baby it with constant watering and fertilizer, it will grow big and green and leafy and give you absolutely nothing. No flowers. No fruit. Just leaves.

If your tree is leafy with no flowers, it is getting too much nitrogen. Cut back on the fertilizer. Let it struggle a little. Stress triggers fruiting.

Prune lightly to shape the tree, but do not overdo it. Heavy pruning stresses citrus and delays fruiting.

And here is the thing nobody prepares you for: fresh citrus from your backyard does not taste like store-bought citrus.

It is sweeter. Juicier. The flavor is concentrated and bright. You will squeeze a lime into your drink and stop mid-pour because the smell alone is that strong. You will zest a lemon and the oils will coat your fingers and you will smell it for hours.

Store-bought citrus tastes watered down after that. Like it forgot what it was supposed to be.

In the Kitchen

6. Citrus

Zest it. Squeeze it. Slice it. Citrus is the MVP of the kitchen.

Make lemon water, limeade, marinades, salad dressings. Preserve the rinds in sugar or salt for later use.

I freeze juice in ice cube trays and drop them into teas or recipes later. Fresh citrus on demand, anytime.

Did You Know?

Citrus grown in pots often fruits faster than in the ground. Especially lemons and limes.

And dwarf varieties are made just for containers. Meyer lemon, Key lime, Calamondin orange. All of them thrive in pots and fruit like crazy if you treat them right.

Figure 11 Lemons in Pots

7. Asparagus

The Crop That Tests Your Patience... and Your Labeling Skills

After watching way too many garden videos, I just knew: I can grow asparagus.

So I went for it. Dug a trench, followed the instructions, and planted it behind the blackberries.

A few weeks later, boom. Progress. Shoots started popping up.

Then a month later... nothing.

I figured maybe I picked the wrong variety for my zone. Maybe asparagus does not like Florida. Maybe I did something wrong.

But turns out it was thriving.

Now here is the twist.

My husband went to clean the garden one day. He did not know what I had planted. Because yes, I still had that bad habit of not labeling anything.

And he thought the asparagus was weeds.

Smashed. Gone. Ferrari-level garden wreckage.

Round two? I planted them in a raised bed. Marked it. Left room. And guess what? They are thriving.

First harvest is coming soon. And this time, nobody is touching it.

7. Asparagus

Best Planting Time

January to March in Florida. Plant crowns when the soil starts to warm but before it gets too hot.

How to Plant It

Figure 12 Asparagus crowns

Start with asparagus crowns. Those are baby roots, not seeds. Crowns give you a head start. You can grow asparagus from seeds, but it takes even longer. Trust me. Use crowns.

Dig a trench 6 to 8 inches deep. Plant the crowns with the buds facing up. Do not plant them upside down. The buds are the little bumps that will become your asparagus spears.

Cover with 2 inches of soil. Then as the shoots grow, gradually fill in the trench. Do not bury them all at once. Let them grow up, then add more soil. Repeat until the trench is level with the ground.

In raised beds, space crowns 12 to 18 inches apart. Asparagus spreads. Give it room.

And here is the most important part: **label it.** I do not care if you write it with a stick. Just let someone know it is asparagus. Not weeds. Asparagus.

Can It Grow in a Pot?

Not really. Asparagus wants deep roots and space to spread. It is a perennial. It stays in the ground for years. It does not want to be confined.

7. Asparagus

If you absolutely must grow it in a pot, use a very deep container. At least 18 to 24 inches deep. And only one crown per pot. Even then, it will not be as productive as it would be in the ground.

Save yourself the hassle. Plant it in the ground or in a raised bed.

How to Care for It

Figure 13 - 2nd Year Asparagus

Asparagus wants full sun. Six to eight hours daily.

Keep it moist but not soggy during the growing season. Asparagus does not like to dry out completely, but it also does not like wet feet. Balance.

Your soil needs to be well-draining and rich with compost. Asparagus roots go deep. At least 12 to 18 inches. So loosen the soil before you plant. If your soil is compacted or heavy clay, the roots cannot spread and the plant will struggle.

Mulch around the plants to hold moisture and keep weeds down. Weeds compete with asparagus for nutrients and water. Do not let them win.

Feed it with a balanced fertilizer in early spring and again after harvest season. Asparagus is a heavy feeder. It needs nutrients to build strong roots and produce spears year after year.

Pests and Problems

Keep an eye out for asparagus beetles. They are small, metallic-looking bugs that lay eggs on the spears. Hand-pick them and destroy the eggs. Do not let them multiply.

In winter, remove old fern growth. The ferns die back naturally, but leaving them in the bed gives pests a place to overwinter. Cut them down and toss them.

If rust becomes a problem (orange spots on the ferns), rotate planting beds. Do not plant asparagus in the same spot year after year if rust shows up.

When to Harvest

This is the hard part.

You cannot harvest much the first year. Maybe a few spears. But resist the urge to take more. The plant needs to build strength.

Year two, you can do a small harvest. Cut for 2 to 3 weeks, then stop.

Year three, you can go full harvest. Cut for 6 to 8 weeks.

After that, asparagus can produce for 15 to 20 years. Once it is established, it keeps giving.

Harvest when the spears are 6 to 8 inches tall and about as thick as your finger. Cut them at soil level or snap them off by hand. Do not wait until they get too tall and fern out. Once they start opening at the top, they are too tough to eat.

What No One Tells You

Asparagus dies back in summer. The spears stop coming. The ferns grow tall and feathery. Do not panic. That is normal.

The ferns are feeding the roots. They are storing energy for next year's harvest. Do not cut them down until they turn brown in late fall or winter.

You cannot harvest much the first year. Let it build strength. Patience now equals years of harvest later.

And fresh asparagus from your backyard tastes different. Tender, fresh, and slightly grassy in a good way. Way more flavor than store-bought.

When it is roasted with garlic or grilled with olive oil? Next level.

In the Kitchen

Roast asparagus with garlic and olive oil at 400°F for 15 minutes. Or sauté it with butter and lemon. You can also grill it and shave fresh Parmesan on top.

It is great with eggs, pasta, or chopped into cold salads.

7. Asparagus

Toni's Tip

Give asparagus its own space. Label it. And tell everybody in the house to leave it alone.

You waited too long for those little spears to come in just to lose them in a weekend cleanup.

Did You Know?

Asparagus is one of the only perennial vegetables you can grow in Florida. Once it is happy, it keeps giving for decades.

And it is high in folate and vitamin K. Great for digestion, anti-inflammatory, a natural diuretic. Full of antioxidants and supports liver health.

8. Papaya

The Plant That Tastes Like Home

I grew up watching papaya go into legim. Not as something fancy or special, just part of the pot.

My mom did not explain it or make a big deal about it. She peeled it, cut it, and kept moving. That is kitchen knowledge you learn by standing close, not by being taught.

So when I started growing papaya myself, it felt familiar from the start.

The first time I harvested one, I did not go for a breakfast bowl. I put it straight into legim, and it tasted exactly like home.

That is when I knew papaya belonged in my garden.

What is Legim?

8. Papaya

Figure 14 Haitian Legim with white rice

Legim is a traditional Haitian vegetable stew. You take whatever vegetables you have, cook them down with epis (Haitian seasoning base of herbs, garlic, and peppers), and mash or blend until everything comes together into a thick savory base.

Green papaya goes in legim the same way you might use chayote or squash. It softens, stretches the pot, and blends into the flavor.

If you did not grow up with it, think of it as a slow-cooked, well-seasoned vegetable mash that you eat with rice. Simple, comforting, filling.

Simple Haitian Legim Base (The Foundation):

Prep: Peel and cube one medium green papaya (or use squash or chayote). Chop half an onion, one carrot, and one bell pepper.

Season: In a large pot, sauté your vegetables with epis and a tablespoon of cooking oil.

Cook Down: Add water, a few sprigs of thyme, and a scotch bonnet pepper (whole, do not cut it). Bring to a boil, then reduce heat, cover, and let simmer for at least 45 minutes until all the vegetables are fork tender and falling apart.

Finish: Remove the whole thyme sprigs and the scotch bonnet. Use a large spoon or masher to crush the vegetables until the sauce is thick and smooth. Serve hot over rice.

8. Papaya

The Practical Plant

Papaya grows fast. Once it is settled, it shoots up quick. It grows up, not out, so it does not take much yard space.

It is a practical plant. It supports the house.

You get multiple uses from one tree:

Fruit for breakfast and snacks

Green fruit for legim and savory dishes

Seeds you can dry and grind like pepper

Leaves for functional tea if needed

Best Planting Time

March through August. Papaya needs warm soil and sun to thrive. Frost will kill it, so plant once the weather is settled and hot.

How to Plant It

Choose a sunny spot. Full sun. All day if you can give it.

Plant with the root base slightly above soil level. Do not bury it deep. Papaya hates wet ground. If the base sits too low, it will rot.

Water steadily while young, then cut back once it is established. Mulch the base to hold moisture without waterlogging the roots.

Do not plant in low areas where rainwater pools. Papaya will sit in that water and rot from the roots up.

Can You Grow It in a Pot?

Yes, but it needs a huge pot. Twenty to thirty gallons minimum.

Papaya grows fast and tall. If you start it in a small pot, you will need to upsize or transplant later. So just go big from the start or plant it in the ground.

Male, Female, Hermaphrodite Trees

This part matters. Not every papaya tree will fruit.

Male trees only make flowers. No fruit. Ever.

Female trees need another tree nearby to pollinate and fruit.

Hermaphrodite trees [14]fruit on their own. This is what you want.

If you are growing from seed, you will not know which one you have until it flowers. So plant three to five seeds. Wait for them to flower. Keep the one that fruits the way you want. Remove the rest.

Do not hesitate. Do not keep male trees hoping they will fruit. They will not. Your garden is not a museum.

How to Care for It

Papaya loves full sun, heat, and moderate watering. Florida gives all of that naturally.

Water young trees regularly until they are established. Once they are growing strong, cut back. Too much water rots the roots.

Feed with compost or a balanced fertilizer every few months. Papaya is a fast grower and a heavy feeder. It needs nutrients to keep producing.

Mulch around the base, but do not pile it against the trunk. The trunk needs air.

When to Harvest

The skin begins to turn yellow. That is your first sign.

Press gently near the top. If it has a slight give, it is ready.

If you wait for full yellow, the birds will get it first. Take it earlier and finish ripening inside on the counter.

Green papaya for legim? Pick it while it is still hard and green. Peel it, remove the seeds, cut it into chunks, and cook it.

---

[14] **Hermaphrodite (Self-Pollinating):** In gardening terms, this refers to a plant that possesses both male and female reproductive organs within the same flower. These trees are "independent"—they don't require pollen from a different tree to set fruit, which makes them perfect for small Florida backyards where you don't have the space for an orchard.

Green Papaya and Ripe Papaya in the Kitchen

Green Papaya: Use when the fruit is still firm and not sweet. Peel it, remove the seeds, cut it into chunks, and cook it in legim, soups, or stir fry. It takes on flavor and becomes soft.

Ripe Papaya: Cut it, spoon it, squeeze lime, and serve. Use in smoothies, fruit bowls, or just eat as is.

Seeds: Dry and grind. The taste is sharp, strong, and similar to black pepper. Use in moderation. Seeds can be strong and should be avoided during pregnancy.

Leaves: Used for tea in some households to support recovery and digestion. Not a flavor tea. A functional tea. Always cook or dry leaves before use. Raw leaves can irritate the stomach.

Health Benefits

Fruit: Rich in Vitamin C, A, and E. Supports immunity and skin health. Packed with fiber and antioxidants. Great for digestion and gut balance. Contains the papain enzyme which helps break down protein, reduces bloating, and fights inflammation.

Leaves: Used in herbal teas to help with digestion and immune support. Believed to help regulate blood sugar and reduce menstrual pain. May support liver function and reduce inflammation.

Seeds: Natural anti-parasitic properties in small amounts. May support kidney and liver detox. Dry and crush for seasoning. They have a slightly spicy, pepper-like flavor.

Common Mistakes

Overwatering. Papaya does not like wet feet. Too much water rots the roots.

Keeping male trees hoping they will fruit. They will not. Remove them.

Planting too close to walkways. Papaya grows tall and drops fruit. Give it space.

Waiting too long to harvest. Birds will get it before you do.

8. Papaya

Toni's Tip

If your papaya grows too tall to reach the fruit, cut the trunk halfway and lay it sideways. Papaya will regrow new shoots from the stem.

It is not a fragile plant. It rebounds.

And do not sleep on papaya leaves or seeds. We grow for more than just fruit around here. Start with one seed, and you might end up with a whole food medicine cabinet.

Did You Know?

Papaya enzymes are used in natural meat tenderizers. That same compound (papain) helps break down tough proteins in your body and food.

Figure 15 Our One Year Papaya

Garden Reflection

Write down one ingredient from your childhood kitchen that still feels like home to you. Even if you have not used it in years. Just acknowledge it.

8. Papaya

9. Pigeon Peas

More Than Beans, This Plant Has Power

So I'm over at my parents' house, just giving my dad the rundown of what we've been growing. You know, showing off a little. Like, "Look, Daddy, we've got beans!"

Now I grew up in a Haitian household where "rice and beans" was dinner at least twice a week. The flavor, the texture, the way it soaks up epis? Classic.

But in the middle of my proud garden moment, my dad looks at the plant and goes:

"Mwen pa bezwen pwa a. Se fèy la ki pi fò."

("I don't care about the beans. The leaves. That's where the power is.")

And just like that, he kept walking.

So I followed up. Did my research. And whew. Turns out this plant is not just food. It is medicine. The leaves, the pods, the whole thing.

Pigeon peas are not just for Sunday plates. They are a survival crop. A healing plant.

And now I look at it totally different.

9. Pigeon Peas

Figure 16 Pigeon peas planted next to Sugarcanes

What Makes This Plant Different

Most people grow pigeon peas for the beans. And yes, the beans are good. They are protein-rich, filling, and taste incredible in rice and peas.

But the leaves? The leaves are where the real value is.

Pigeon pea leaves are used in traditional medicine across the Caribbean, Africa, and Asia. They are anti-inflammatory, support digestion, and help regulate blood sugar. People brew them into tea for respiratory issues, fevers, and to strengthen the immune system.

The whole plant is useful. The beans feed you. The leaves heal you. And the roots fix nitrogen in the soil, making your garden healthier for whatever you plant next.

This is not just a crop. This is a workhorse.

When to Plant

March through July. Pigeon peas love heat and full sun. The warmer it gets, the better they grow.

Do not plant them in winter. They will just sit there waiting for warmth.

9. Pigeon Peas

How to Plant

Direct sow seeds in the ground or in large pots. About 1 inch deep.

Space them at least 2 to 3 feet apart. Pigeon peas grow into tall, bushy plants. Six to ten feet tall. They need room.

They will sprout within 1 to 2 weeks and take off fast.

And here is the thing: pigeon peas do not like to be moved. Plant them where you want them to stay. Do not start them in small pots thinking you will transplant later. They do not transplant well. Their roots do not like being disturbed.

In a Pot? Only If You Go Big

Yes, you can grow pigeon peas in a pot. But it needs to be big. At least 15 to 20 gallons.

Pigeon peas grow tall like mini trees. If the pot is too small, the plant will get root-bound and struggle.

If you have yard space, plant them in the ground. Let them stretch.

What They Need

Full sun all day. Pigeon peas are sun worshippers. Shade makes them weak and unproductive.

Water deeply once or twice a week once they are established. Young plants need consistent moisture, but mature plants are drought-tolerant. They can handle dry spells better than most crops.

The soil just needs to drain well. Slightly sandy is fine. Pigeon peas are not picky. They tolerate a range of soils as long as water does not sit around the roots.

Add compost before planting to improve fertility. But after that, you do not need much fertilizer. Pigeon peas fix their own nitrogen. They pull nitrogen from the air and store it in their roots. So they actually feed the soil instead of depleting it.

What Can Go Wrong

Caterpillars and aphids are the main pests. If you see them, use neem oil or insecticidal soap. Do not wait. They multiply fast.

Fungal wilts can show up if the soil stays too wet. Rotate crops. Do not plant pigeon peas in the same spot year after year if you have had wilt issues.

When to Harvest

Fresh green pods: 2 to 3 months after planting. Pick them when the pods are plump and the peas inside are tender. Use them fresh like you would use edamame or snap peas.

Dried beans: 4 to 6 months. Wait until the pods turn brown and dry on the plant. Shell them and store the dried beans for cooking later.

Leaves: Anytime the plant is growing. Pick young, tender leaves for tea or cooking. Do not strip the whole plant. Just take what you need and let it keep growing.

The Leaves Are the Power

My dad was right.

The leaves are anti-inflammatory, support digestion, help regulate blood sugar, and strengthen the immune system. People brew them into tea for respiratory issues, fevers, and overall wellness.

You can also cook the young leaves like you would cook spinach or collard greens. Sauté them with garlic and oil, or add them to soups and stews.

The leaves are the part most people overlook. But in traditional medicine, they are the most valued part of the plant.

In the Kitchen

The Beans:

Cook dried pigeon peas just like you would cook black beans or kidney beans. Soak them overnight, then simmer with epis, thyme, and a scotch bonnet pepper. Serve over rice.

9. Pigeon Peas

Figure 17 Rice and Peas

Fresh green peas cook faster. No soaking needed. Just shell them and add them to stir-fries, curries, or rice dishes.

The Leaves:

Brew young leaves into tea. Steep them in hot water for 10 to 15 minutes. Drink it plain or add honey and lime.

Or cook them like greens. Sauté with garlic, onions, and a little oil. Add them to soups or stews.

What No One Tells You

Pigeon peas grow tall. Six to ten feet. If you plant them near a fence or walkway, they will take over. Give them space.

They reseed themselves. If you let the pods dry and drop, new plants will sprout next season. You might not even need to replant.

They fix nitrogen in the soil. So after you harvest, cut the plant down but leave the roots in the ground. They will break down and feed the soil for your next crop.

And the plant is not just food. It is medicine. The beans feed you. The leaves heal you. The roots feed your soil.

This is a survival crop.

Toni's Tip

Listen to your elders. They know things you have not learned yet.

I was out here proud of my beans. My dad saw the whole plant.

Now I grow pigeon peas for the leaves just as much as the beans. And I look at every plant in my garden a little differently because of it.

Did You Know?

Pigeon peas are one of the oldest cultivated crops in the world. They have been grown for over 3,500 years in Africa, Asia, and the Caribbean.

They are drought-tolerant, heat-loving, and improve soil quality. In many parts of the world, they are considered a staple survival crop because they thrive in tough conditions and provide both food and medicine.

10. Guava

A Backyard Perfume. A Miami Childhood. A Whole Lotta Fruit.

You cannot say you are from Miami and never heard of guava pastelitos. Guava and cheese, that flaky pastry? That is childhood. That is joy. That is home.

So when we had the chance to grow a guava tree in our yard? Oh, I was excited. Real excited.

What I did not realize was how much fruit it would give me. And all at once.

But did that stop me? Nope.

Guava is one of those childhood memory fruits that brings you straight to your happy place.

The smell? Whew. It is like having your own personal perfume line growing in the backyard. Tropical, floral, sweet. It will hit you before you even see the fruit.

Let me tell you, once ours started producing, I was up to my eyeballs in guava. I made guava jam, guava juice, guava cake, guava cookies... you name it.

This tree does not play.

When to Plant

March through August. Guava loves heat and will grow fast in Florida's climate.

10. Guava

How to Plant

Choose a sunny spot with room to grow. Guava trees can reach 10 to 20 feet tall.

Dig a hole twice as wide as the rootball and plant slightly above ground level. Do not bury the trunk. Guava does not like wet feet.

Water deeply after planting and mulch around the base. But do not pile mulch against the trunk. Give it air.

Space multiple trees at least 10 feet apart. They spread.

Start small. Even a 3-gallon pot. Guava will take off. And do not wait too long to prune. They grow fast.

In a Pot? Yes, Especially Dwarf Varieties

Use a 20 to 25 gallon container with well-draining soil. Keep it pruned for size control.

Guava in pots produces just as well as in the ground if you give it enough room and sun.

What It Needs

Full sun all day. Guava is a sun worshipper.

Deep water 2 to 3 times a week during hot months. Once it is established, it can handle some drought, but consistent watering means more fruit.

The soil needs to be loamy and well-draining. Mix in compost or organic matter before planting.

Feed it with a balanced fruit tree fertilizer every 6 to 8 weeks during the growing season.

Prune in spring to keep it full and productive. Guava grows fast. If you do not prune, it will turn into a jungle.

What Can Go Wrong

Fruit flies are the biggest enemy. They lay eggs in the fruit and ruin it from the inside. Bagging fruit while it is still small helps.

Scale insects love guava. If you see them, scrape them off or use neem oil.

Prune regularly for airflow to reduce fungal diseases. Florida humidity invites fungus, but good airflow helps.

When to Harvest

Two to four years from planting, you will get your first real harvest.

You will know it is ready when:

The skin lightens from green to yellow or blush pink

It softens slightly when you squeeze it

The smell is sweet and strong. Your tree will literally tell on itself.

Pick it when it is ripe or just before. If you wait too long, the fruit flies will get it first.

The Smell That Hits You First

The fragrance is so strong, your whole yard will smell tropical when it is fruiting.

You will walk outside and smell it before you see it. Sweet, floral, like a rose garden crossed with a tropical fruit stand.

Some people plant guava just for the smell. The fruit is a bonus.

What No One Tells You

Guavas can fruit multiple times a year in Florida. Spring, summer, sometimes even fall. You will have waves of fruit.

They are pest magnets. Keep an eye out for fruit flies and scale.

The fruit can drop all at once. You will have 50 guavas ripe at the same time. Be ready to use or preserve fast.

And the taste? Sweet, floral, slightly tangy, like a tropical fruit met a rose garden. The texture is soft with a little crunch from the seeds. Some varieties are creamy, others more firm, but all of them smell like heaven.

In the Kitchen: How to Really Use Your Guava Harvest

Slice it fresh, blend into juice, bake into cakes, or make guava paste and jam.

But when you have 50 guavas all at once, you need a plan.

Guava and Cheese Pastelitos (My Go-To):

These are simple, flaky pastries. Sweet, creamy, and fast to make.

You will need:

- Puff pastry sheets (store-bought works fine)
- Guava paste (sliceable, not jam)
- Cream cheese
- 1 egg (for brushing)

How to make them:

1. Preheat your oven to 375°F.
2. Cut the puff pastry into squares, about 3x3 inches.
3. Add a small piece of guava paste and a spoon of cream cheese to the center.
4. Fold into triangles or rectangles and press the edges with a fork.
5. Brush the tops with a beaten egg.

6. Bake for 20 to 25 minutes or until golden and flaky.
7. Cool slightly. The guava gets lava hot inside.

Optional: Dust with powdered sugar or drizzle with homemade guava syrup.

Homemade Guava Syrup for Pancakes, Drinks, or Ice Cream:

This syrup tastes tropical and tangy. You can make it with ripe guavas, frozen pulp, or even leftover jam.

You will need:

- 4 to 5 ripe guavas (or 1 cup frozen pulp)
- 1 cup sugar or honey
- 1½ cups water
- 1 teaspoon lime juice

How to make it:

1. Chop the guavas and simmer with water for 10 to 15 minutes until soft.
2. Strain through a fine sieve or cheesecloth to get smooth pulp.
3. Add sugar and lime juice to the liquid and simmer again until it thickens slightly (about 8 to 10 minutes).
4. Let cool, then store in a jar in the fridge. It keeps for up to two weeks.

Use this syrup on pancakes, waffles, yogurt, or even as a glaze for roasted meats. Yes, it works there too.

The Whole Plant Is Useful

Fruit: Extremely high in vitamin C. More than oranges. Rich in fiber, helps with digestion. Packed with antioxidants, supports immunity and skin health. Helps regulate blood sugar and boosts heart health.

Leaves: Brewed into teas for digestive issues, coughs, and inflammation. Traditionally used to lower blood sugar. Antibacterial and may support oral health when used as a rinse.

Seeds: Edible, high in fiber. Mild laxative effect (do not overdo it). Some cultures dry and crush seeds for natural remedies.

10. Guava

Toni's Tip

This is a fruit that takes over, in the best way. When it is in season, you are on guava duty.

Have your recipes ready. Have your freezer bags ready. Have your people ready.

And do not forget to share. One guava tree is enough for the whole block.

Did You Know?

One cup of guava can give you over 400% of your daily vitamin C, plus more potassium than a banana.

The leaves? Even studied for their natural antibiotic and antidiarrheal properties.

Figure 18 Our guavas covered in mesh bags

11. Figs

Not My Favorite... But My Husband Would Plant a Whole Orchard

Now listen, I have got to be honest. Figs? Not really my favorite.

But my husband? Whew. If figs were a person, he would marry them. Especially purple figs and that one variety called Little Miss Figgy. He will talk about her until his face turns blue.

This man used to spend so much money at the store buying dried figs, fig bars, fig jam, fig whatever.

So finally I said, "Why don't we just grow the plant?"

Me? I am the jam mom. So even though I am not running out there to eat them fresh, when those figs come in? It is jam season in my kitchen. And that, I love.

Now here is the kicker.

While I was giving my mom a tour of the garden, she walks past the fig tree, glances at it, and goes, "Oh, figs? Good for blood pressure. Helps regulate sugar too."

And just like that, she kept walking. They have a tendency to do that.

Turns out? She was right. And not just about the fruit. The leaves are just as powerful.

This little tree is packing a whole lot more than flavor.

When to Plant

February through June in Florida. Figs like a warm start and plenty of sun.

11. Figs

How to Plant

Choose a sunny spot with room to spread. Fig trees can grow 10 to 20 feet wide.

Plant slightly above ground level in well-draining soil. Do not bury the trunk. Figs do not like wet feet.

Water deeply after planting and mulch around the base. But do not pile mulch against the trunk.

Space multiple trees at least 15 feet apart.

If you are short on space or patience, try a dwarf variety like Little Miss Figgy or Celeste. Perfect for containers and small yards.

In a Pot? Yes, Figs Love Containers

Figs actually do great in pots. Choose a 15 to 25 gallon container and prune yearly to keep them compact and productive.

Container figs fruit faster than in-ground trees. One to two years versus two to three.

What They Need

Full sun. Six to eight hours minimum. The more sun, the sweeter the figs.

Water deeply once a week during dry months. Figs are drought-tolerant once established, but consistent water means better fruit.

The soil needs to be well-draining. Slightly sandy or loamy. Figs are tolerant of poor soils, but they produce better fruit when organic matter is added.

Do not plant in low spots where water collects. Figs will rot.

Feed them lightly in spring and early summer. Figs do better with less fertilizer. Too much nitrogen makes big leafy trees with small fruit.

Prune after fruiting or during dormancy in winter. Pruning keeps them productive and manageable.

What Can Go Wrong

Birds love ripe figs. Netting is essential. Otherwise, you are growing fruit for the birds, not yourself.

Scale insects and nematodes can show up. Beneficial nematodes in the soil help keep populations down.

Keep trees pruned to improve airflow and reduce rust.

And here is the thing nobody warns you about: fig sap (latex) can irritate your skin. Wear gloves if needed during pruning or harvest.

When to Harvest

One to two years for early fruiting in pots. Two to three years in-ground.

Figs ripen in late summer. They do not all ripen at once. You will be picking every few days for weeks.

You will know they are ready when:

The neck starts drooping

The fruit softens slightly

A little sugary drip might show up. That is your "pick me now" sign.

Once they ripen, use them fast. Figs are delicate. They do not last long.

What Mom Was Right About

The fruit is high in fiber. Supports digestion and helps regulate blood sugar levels. Rich in potassium and calcium. Helps manage blood pressure and support bone health. Full of antioxidants. Great for skin, heart, and immune system.

Mildly laxative when eaten in quantity. Do not say I did not warn you.

The leaves? Used in teas or poultices for blood sugar regulation. May improve insulin sensitivity and lower glucose. May naturally help lower blood pressure. Known for anti-inflammatory properties. Supports respiratory and immune health.

Also used topically for skin issues or irritation in some cultures.

The seeds are tiny, edible, and packed with fiber and enzymes. Aid in digestion and help keep things moving.

My mom dropped that knowledge mid-garden tour and kept walking. But she was right.

11. Figs

What No One Tells You

Figs are delicate. Once they ripen, use them fast. They do not keep.

Ants and birds love them. Harvest daily and consider netting. Otherwise, you will lose half your crop.

They drop all their leaves in winter. Do not panic. That is totally normal. They are deciduous. They come back.

And fresh figs taste different than dried figs. They are soft, sweet, and rich. Almost like a mix between a date, a berry, and a pear. The inside is seedy but soft, with a jammy center.

Some people are obsessed. Some (like me) prefer it in pastry form.

In the Kitchen

Fresh figs pair beautifully with goat cheese, balsamic glaze, or prosciutto.

I use them for fig jam. Simmer with lemon juice, sugar, and a little cinnamon until thick and golden. It is dreamy on toast, chicken, or baked into muffins.

My husband eats them fresh. I make the jam. We both win.

Toni's Tip

This one might not be my go-to snack, but it is here to stay.

11. Figs

Grow one for the jam. Grow one for your fig-obsessed husband. And definitely listen when your mom casually drops medical facts mid-tour.

She knows what she is talking about.

Did You Know?

Figs are one of the oldest cultivated crops in history. Grown for over 11,000 years.

And fun fact: they are technically not a fruit, but an inverted flower that you eat from the inside out.

Wild, right?

Best for: Full sun, anyone with a fig-obsessed family member, people who make jam, anyone interested in blood sugar regulation or natural blood pressure support.

12. Lemongrass

We Tried to Kill It... Turns Out, It Was Trying to Heal Us

You know what is wild? I did not realize every plant in this garden had a meaning, a backstory.

But lemongrass? Whew, this one humbled us.

When we moved in, the backyard was empty. No pool. No swing set. No raised beds. Just this big ol' bush smack in the ground.

And let me tell you, we tried our hardest to get rid of it.

We thought it was a weed. We had the lawn guy chop it down. It grew back bigger. I am talking bigger.

We tried digging it out. That thing did not just stay. It fought back. It practically dug us up.

Eventually, we gave up.

Then my cousin came over, looking around, loving the house. And she stops in her tracks and says, "Oh my goodness, you have got lemongrass!"

Lemon what?

She said, "Yes, it is also called Shrenjan or citronella grass. You can make teas, it is calming, it is great for digestion."

I was like, how do you even know this?

We looked it up. She was right.

That bush we were fighting? That "weed" was a healing herb.

Talk about a backyard lesson.

When to Plant

March through September in Florida. Lemongrass loves heat, sun, and room to spread.

How to Plant

Start with a rooted stalk or division from a friend. You cannot grow lemongrass from seeds easily. Get a cutting or buy a starter plant.

Plant it in loose, well-draining soil. Or in a large pot if you want to control the spread. Because lemongrass spreads. Fast.

Space plants at least 2 to 3 feet apart. Give it room.

Water well at planting and mulch around the base.

This plant does not ask for much. But once it loves your yard? It is not going anywhere. So give it its own space.

In a Pot? Honestly, It Might Be Easier

Absolutely. Use a 5 to 10 gallon pot minimum. Trim it back once or twice a year to keep it bushy and manageable.

In the ground, lemongrass will take over. In a pot, you control it.

What It Needs

Full sun. Lemongrass loves heat. The hotter, the better.

Water moderately, especially during dry spells. Once it is established, it can handle some drought, but consistent water keeps it producing.

The soil needs to be loose and well-draining. Add compost if needed. Avoid heavy clay that holds too much water.

Trim the top growth every few months. Use the stalks fresh or freeze them for later.

What Can Go Wrong

Generally pest-resistant. But aphids and spider mites can appear. A strong spray of water or neem oil will manage them.

Keep clumps thinned to prevent fungal issues. If it gets too dense, airflow drops and fungus moves in.

When to Harvest

You can start harvesting once stalks are thick like your finger. Usually 3 to 4 months after planting.

Trim the outer stalks, not the whole plant. The plant keeps growing from the center.

The stalks you use for tea and cooking grow low near the base, not the green grassy tops. Cut low. That is where the flavor is.

What That "Weed" Actually Does

Stalks: Naturally calming. Helps with anxiety and stress. Great for digestion, bloating, and gut health. Antibacterial and antifungal. Supports immune function. Mild pain reliever and fever reducer in traditional medicine.

Leaves: Brewed into teas for sleep, relaxation, and cold relief. May help reduce blood pressure and cholesterol. Used topically (in balms or oils) for joint pain and swelling.

Oil (if distilled): Repels mosquitoes. Used in aromatherapy for focus and calm. Natural anti-inflammatory.

Well, well, they say it repels mosquitoes, but I do not know if they mean Florida mosquitoes or the high-maintenance, extra-stubborn ones. Because honestly? I have not seen it do a thing yet.

What No One Tells You

12. Lemongrass

It multiplies fast. One plant can become 10 by the next year. If you do not contain it, it will spread across your yard.

You can freeze trimmed stalks for future use. They hold their flavor well.

Once it is established, it will return year after year like clockwork. You do not need to replant.

And the taste? Bright, citrusy, slightly minty with a floral twist. It is like lemon... but grown up. It adds depth to teas, soups, stews, and even marinades.

In the Kitchen

To make lemongrass tea, chop 1 to 2 stalks, crush them lightly, and simmer in water for 10 to 15 minutes. Add ginger or mint for extra flavor.

It is also great in broths, curry bases, or even thrown on the grill inside foil packets.

Toni's Tip

Sometimes your biggest blessings come disguised as something you are trying to get rid of.

That "weed" turned out to be a whole healing bush. Now I use it weekly. Tea, steam, marinade, you name it.

Did You Know?

Lemongrass is used in Ayurveda, traditional Chinese medicine, and Caribbean folk healing.

It has been shown to help reduce stress, aid digestion, and may even inhibit bacterial growth.

Best for: Full sun, anyone who wants a low-maintenance perennial herb, people interested in natural teas and healing plants.

13. Loquat

From "Lo-Who?" to Our Favorite After-School Snack

Loquat is new for us. I did not grow up with it. But these past four years? I have fallen in love.

It all started with our neighbor. She has this big loquat tree sitting dead center in her yard. Every year it blooms, flowers, fruits... and nobody touches it. Just sits there like a hidden gem.

One day, I came home after picking up my son from school, and she happened to be outside. She brought us over to the tree and said, "Here, try this."

My son, who chews lemons like candy, loved them.

From that day on, every single afternoon after school, he would run straight to that tree. Pocket full of loquats. Cheeks puffed out. So proud.

Now we have got our own loquat growing. Started from that very same seed. It is still young, so yes... we are still visiting our adopted tree across the street.

But we are on our way.

When to Plant

February through May is your window. Loquats thrive in the mild transition from winter to spring, so get them in the ground before the summer heat really kicks in.

Getting Started

Skip the seeds. If you want fruit that actually tastes like the parent tree, buy a grafted nursery seedling. A seed-grown tree is a total gamble; it will take years longer to fruit, and you have no guarantee on the quality. Dig a hole twice as wide as your pot, and make sure you plant it slightly above the soil line—do not bury the trunk. Water it deeply, throw down some mulch to keep those roots cool, and give it room. These trees spread, so keep them at least 15 feet away from buildings or other trees.

The "Pot" Strategy

You can keep a loquat in a 15 to 25-gallon pot for the first few years, provided you keep it in full sun and prune it to stay compact. But let's be honest: this tree eventually wants to stretch its legs. If you want a real, heavy-producing tree, get it into the ground.

What It Needs

Full sun is the goal—the more light it gets, the more fruit you'll harvest. While it's young, keep it hydrated, but once it's established, it's surprisingly tough. Just remember that "tough" doesn't mean "swamp-loving." Loquats hate wet feet; if the soil doesn't drain well, you will rot the roots. Amend your soil with plenty of compost, prune it lightly right after you harvest to keep the shape clean, and feed it with a balanced fruit fertilizer a couple of times during the spring and summer.

Troubleshooting

Keep an eye out for scale insects that like to cluster on the stems; you can scrape them off or use a little neem oil to get them under control. Watch for fire blight, which makes branches look like they've been scorched black. If you see it, cut those branches back to clean wood immediately. And keep the netting handy—the birds know exactly when these are ripe, and they will absolutely beat you to them if you aren't careful.

The Harvest

If you bought a grafted tree, you'll be eating fruit in two to five years. The real beauty of the loquat is that it produces in late winter and early spring—a time when almost nothing else is happening in the Florida garden. It fills the gap perfectly. Look for fruit that has turned a deep orange or yellow and feels slightly soft to the touch. It should pull off the branch with a gentle tug. This fruit ripens fast and waits for no one, so keep an eye on it daily. Once it's ready, pick it and eat it—or get it into the kitchen to preserve it

The Fruit, The Leaves, The Whole Tree

Fruit: High in vitamin A and antioxidants. Supports vision and skin health. Good source of potassium and fiber. Natural source of pectin, which supports gut health and reduces cholesterol. Contains compounds that may support liver health and reduce inflammation.

Leaves: Brewed as tea for cough, asthma, and inflammation relief. Used in traditional medicine to help regulate blood sugar. Natural antioxidant and immune booster. May support liver detox and reduce oxidative stress.

Seeds: Not typically eaten due to mild toxicity. Just spit them out like my son does.

Loquat leaves are used in Japanese kampo medicine[15], Haitian herbal blends, and across Caribbean and Asian cultures for their ability to soothe lungs, reduce inflammation, and regulate blood sugar.

What No One Tells You

Loquat trees fruit early. Right when nothing else is producing. Mid-winter to early spring. That alone makes it worth planting.

The fruit ripens fast, so be ready to eat or preserve.

Birds will find it before you do. Netting helps.

---

[15] Japanese Kampo is a traditional system of herbal medicine that originated in China but was refined and adapted over centuries within Japan to fit local needs. Think of it as a highly structured, evidence-based approach to herbal healing.
Unlike some other holistic practices that focus heavily on individual "mystery" herbs, Kampo is built on classic, time-tested formulas—specific combinations of plants, roots, and minerals that are designed to treat a person's *pattern* of symptoms rather than just a single ailment.

13. Loquat

It is ornamental, evergreen, and gorgeous even when not fruiting. The leaves are big, leathery, and tropical-looking. The tree adds beauty to your yard year-round.

And the taste? Like an apricot and mango had a juicy baby with a hint of citrus. It would be called Loquat. (Do not name your baby Loquat, haha)

It is sweet but not overpowering. Soft and slightly tart when under-ripe. You can eat it fresh off the tree or turn it into jams, syrups, or even pie filling.

In the Kitchen

Eat it fresh. Blend into smoothies. Or stew with sugar and ginger for a quick jam.

You can also freeze the pulp for later or mix it into oatmeal, yogurt, or baking.

Figure 19 Our neighbor's Loquat tree

14. Miracle Berry

The Tiny Fruit That Turns Sour into Sweet (Literally)

My husband's pride and joy. He told me all about this little fruit that could change how things taste, and I'm thinking: *okay, what now?* A few years ago, we finally tried the "Miracle Berry Challenge." A little red berry, a slice of lemon, a slice of lime... and suddenly? Boom. Instant lemonade.

It was like flipping a switch. Sour turned into candy; acid turned into sweetness. Everything we tried after that—vinegar, goat cheese, green smoothies—it all tasted like dessert. Now, our kids walk out to the garden thinking this is Willy Wonka's backyard. They'll eat a miracle berry and suddenly believe they can conquer kale, Brussels sprouts, or anything else green.

How the Magic Works The berry itself is mildly sweet and tart, but the real show starts afterward. It contains a natural compound called miraculin[16]. Once you eat the berry, that miraculin binds to your taste buds and literally hijacks your perception, making sour things taste like pure sugar for up to an hour. Yes, it really works. And yes, your kids will want to do this every single day.

---

[16] **Miraculin** is a unique glycoprotein found in the fruit of the *Synsepalum dulcificum* plant, commonly known as the "miracle berry." It is famous for its bizarre and fascinating effect on human taste buds: it makes sour foods, like lemons or limes, taste incredibly sweet.

14. Miracle Berry

Growing Your Own Miracle berry is a slow grower, but a rewarding one. Because it's a tropical native, it's obsessed with acidity. If you plant it in our standard Florida dirt, it will struggle. You need to use a container filled with high-quality pine bark or peat moss to keep that soil pH low. It also prefers filtered light or partial shade; put this in the harsh Florida full sun, and it will scorch. Keep it moist but never soaked—it hates dry roots, but it hates "wet feet" even more. If you're in the ground, mulch it heavily and have a frost blanket ready to go. This plant does not do cold.

What Can Go Wrong Pests usually leave it alone, but watch for spider mites if you bring it indoors during the winter. If the leaves start turning yellow, it's almost always a soil pH issue—add more peat moss. And seriously: protect it from frost. If temperatures dip below 50°F, get that pot inside or get it covered.

The Harvest Wait You're looking at a three-to-four-year wait before you see your first berry. I know—that's a long time. But once it starts, it fruits multiple times a year if you keep it warm and happy. The berries are small, bright red, and about the size of a coffee bean. Pick them when they're soft and fully colored.

The Challenge Want a fun party trick? Set up a "tasting night" with sour and bitter foods and watch your guests lose their minds. Try it before a charcuterie board, a vinegar-based shrub, or even just plain old citrus. One word of warning: do not try this right after brushing your teeth. Trust me.

This plant is essentially a science experiment that actually works. It comes from West Africa and has a wild history, it was even once banned in the U.S. because the sugar industry saw it as a threat. Today, it's a staple in high-end Japanese culinary circles. It's one of the only plants that lets you trick your brain naturally, without adding a single grain of actual sugar.

Pro-Tip: Plant this near your blueberries. They share the same obsession with acidic soil, so you can amend your dirt once and keep both plants happy.

15. Ashwagandha

The Stress Buster You Can Grow at Home

Now Ashwagandha... does not that name just sound so... pretty?

You cannot just say it loud and fast. You gotta whisper it: *Ashwagandha...*

That is how it makes you feel.

I first learned about it through my husband. He is our in-house health fanatic. Supplements, powders, you name it. He was popping Ashwagandha pills like they were going out of style.

So for Father's Day, I thought, "Why not grow the real thing?"

I built him his very own raised bed. Yes, his garden space. And planted all the things he was taking in capsule form.

When those Ashwagandha seeds went in the ground? Something happened.

This man became a full-blown gardener. He went from planting fruit trees to dropping watermelon seeds, cucumbers, even weeding with pride.

Look at that.

What It Actually Is

15. Ashwagandha

Ashwagandha is a root. A powerful one. Used in Ayurvedic medicine[17] for over 3,000 years.

You do not eat this one like a fruit. It is more of a super root you dry, steep, and sip. Or grind into powders.

The roots are what is typically used. They taste earthy. Very earthy. Like a strong herbal tea with bitter notes.

Store-bought Ashwagandha? You have had it. But homegrown? That is next level.

When to Plant

Late spring through summer. Once the soil is warm.

Ashwagandha needs warm soil to germinate. Think 70 to 85°F.

Harvest before winter hits, or overwinter in containers if you are in a colder part of Florida.

What It Needs

Full sun all day. Ashwagandha loves heat.

Sandy or loamy soil with good drainage. pH 7.5 to 8.0. It does best in slightly alkaline conditions. Avoid overly rich soil. It prefers lean ground.

Minimal water. Ashwagandha is drought-tolerant. Perfect for Florida heat. Water when you plant it, then back off. Let it fend for itself.

Do not fertilize heavily. This plant does not need it. Too much nitrogen makes leafy plants with weak roots. You want strong roots.

Harvest roots after 6 to 8 months, once the leaves yellow and the plant starts to die back.

What Can Go Wrong

[17] **Ayurvedic medicine** is one of the world's oldest holistic healing systems, developed thousands of years ago in India. The word itself comes from the Sanskrit terms *ayur* (life) and *veda* (knowledge), and it operates on the belief that health and wellness depend on a delicate balance between your mind, body, and spirit.

Mostly pest-free. But flea beetles may chew the leaves. Use floating row covers early on to protect young plants.

Rotate location yearly to prevent root rot. Do not plant Ashwagandha in the same spot year after year.

And here is the thing: if you overwater or over-fertilize, the plant will struggle. It does not want to be pampered. It wants lean soil, hot sun, and minimal fuss.

When to Harvest

Six to eight months after planting, the leaves will start to yellow and the plant will die back. That is your signal.

Dig up the roots. Wash them. Dry them in a warm, dry spot for a few weeks until they are brittle.

You can harvest leaves earlier for tea, but the magic is in the roots.

What It Does for You

You can harvest the leaves for a calming tea, but the root is what really supports adrenal function, helps with sleep, and keeps your stress levels in check. The name actually comes from the Sanskrit *ashva* for "horse" and *gandha* for "smell," because they say it gives you the strength of one—but don't worry, it won't make you smell like a stable.

Figure 20 Ashwagandha Roots

15. Ashwagandha

In the Kitchen (Or Medicine Cabinet)

This is not one you chop into salad. This one is for infusions, teas, and tinctures.

Dry the roots after harvesting. Grind into powder for smoothies or homemade supplements.

Boil pieces of the root to make calming bedtime tea.

Store the dried roots in a jar. They will last for months.

Did You Know?

Ashwagandha has been used in Ayurvedic medicine for over 3,000 years.

It is one of the most studied adaptogenic herbs in the world. Adaptogens help your body handle stress.

And the roots? They contain compounds called withanolides[18], which are responsible for most of the health benefits.

---

[18] Think of **withanolides** as the "engine" inside the Ashwagandha plant. They are a group of naturally occurring compounds that act as the plant's active ingredients—the parts responsible for almost all those stress-relieving and health-boosting benefits we talk about.
When you take a supplement or drink an Ashwagandha root tea, your body is interacting with these specific compounds to help regulate your system.

16. Shampoo Ginger

Now, this is one of those plants you grow just because you can. I mean, where else are you going to see shampoo oozing out of a flower? That is right! This one is for your hair, not your plate. When the red, pinecone-looking flower fills up with juice, you can squeeze it right onto your head like nature's own conditioner. My kids call it the "squishy shampoo plant," and they are obsessed with pressing the cones to see the clear, slippery liquid gush out. You grow this, and suddenly you're the wizard of the neighborhood. Hawaiians call it *Awapuhi*, and it's been used for centuries as a natural cleanser and scalp soother. It's antibacterial, it smells like a spa day mixed with Sunday afternoon naps, and honestly, even the fancy commercial brands use extracts from it.

Getting it started

16. Shampoo Ginger

You cannot grow this one from seeds, so start with rhizomes[19]—just like you would with regular ginger or turmeric. Wait for spring to early summer when the soil is warm and humid, then bury them shallow in rich, well-draining soil. Do not bury them deep; just cover them lightly and give them a good layer of mulch. This plant loves a bit of protection, so keep it in partial shade or dappled sun. If you put it in the full blazing Florida sun all day, it's going to scorch. Keep the soil consistently moist, but don't drown it. If you're using a pot, go big—at least 15 to 20 gallons—because this beauty loves to spread. You'll end up with more plants than you started with in a few years, which is a great excuse to share them with friends.

Keeping it happy

Shampoo ginger is pretty trouble-free, but it does have its preferences. It wants rich, loamy soil with plenty of compost or aged manure mixed in. Every six to eight weeks, give it a little boost with a balanced fertilizer. The biggest thing to watch for is "wet feet." While it loves moisture, it hates sitting in a swamp, so avoid low spots in the yard where water collects, or you'll be dealing with root rot. If you keep it tidy by cutting back the flower heads after they dry out, the plant will reward you with even more growth.

Harvesting your own shampoo

It takes about nine to twelve months for those beautiful red cones to appear. Once they're plump and full of liquid, you're ready. You don't have to pull the whole flower off, just give the cone a gentle squeeze, catch the clear juice, and leave the cone on the plant so it can keep producing for you. It's gold for a dry or itchy scalp. You can even mix the juice with a little aloe vera gel for a leave-in conditioner you can use right after gardening or on the kids' curls. Trust me, it works.

A few things to keep in mind

This is a perennial in our Florida heat, so plant it once and it'll keep coming back. The kids are going to be obsessed with it, be prepared for them to squeeze those cones every single day if you let them. And if your neighbors ask what that plant is? You get to look them right in the eye and say, "Oh, that? That's just my shampoo plant." They'll look at you like you just changed the gam

---

[19] A horizontal underground stem that spreads out and sends up shoots above and roots below. This is how ginger, turmeric, and bananas grow.

17. Passionfruit

The Backyard Vine That Took Over (But Was So Worth It)

The flavor is a tropical punch that hits you with tangy-sweet citrus and floral notes. Inside that hard shell is a jelly-like pulp packed with seeds, juicy, aromatic, and just bursting with flavor. Whether you scoop it into yogurt, stir it into tea, or blend it into a fresh *ji grenadia* [20] like we did back in Haiti, it's an instant tropical upgrade.

I learned the hard way that you don't mess with this vine; I once tried to move a mature one and it dropped every single fruit in protest. Now, I just give it a sturdy trellis, prune it back regularly so it doesn't smother my other plants, and let it do its thing. Every time I scoop out that pulp, I'm 12 years old again, sitting at my family's table. That memory alone makes the pruning worth it.

---

[20] "Ji grenadia" is Haitian Creole for **passionfruit juice**

Getting it in the ground

Wait until the danger of frost is long gone, late spring or early summer is perfect. Passionfruit loves heat and light, so pick a spot in full sun, but make sure it has a serious structure to climb. I'm talking about a heavy-duty fence, a sturdy arbor, or a custom trellis. Do not plant this on a weak gate or a decorative piece of lattice; this vine grows fast and gets heavy, and it *will* pull a weak structure down. Use rich, well-draining soil with a good amount of compost mixed in. If you have the space, plant two vines. Many varieties need a partner to pollinate, and if you only plant one, you'll get beautiful flowers but zero fruit.

Keeping the dragon tamed

This plant is aggressive. If you don't prune it, it will turn your backyard into a tangled, impossible-to-manage jungle. Give it space away from delicate plants because it will smother anything in its path. Water it deeply, but let the top few inches of soil dry out between waterings—passionfruit hates having "wet feet." Mulch the roots to keep them cool during our brutal Florida summers, and keep an eye out for pests like aphids or mites. A little neem oil goes a long way, and pruning for airflow keeps the fungus away.

Figure 21 Passion fruit on a trellis

The harvest and the ritual

It takes about a year or two to see your first fruit. Once it starts, the rule is simple: be patient. The fruit ripens on the vine and then drops when it's ready. Don't pluck them early, or they won't be sweet. Check the ground under your trellis daily during the season. You'll know they're ready when the color deepens and the shell starts to get those little wrinkles—that's when the flavor is at its peak. They don't last long after they fall, so gather them up and get them into the kitchen.

A few things to keep in mind

The flowers are absolutely stunning—purple and white with these wild, intricate patterns that look like they belong in a nature documentary. They were actually named by missionaries who thought they represented the Passion of Christ, which is where the name comes from. Just remember that the leaves aren't for eating raw; they're traditionally used in teas to help with anxiety and sleep. And if you're looking to make that classic *ji grenadia*, just blend the pulp and seeds, strain it, and sweeten it to your liking. It's not just a drink; it's a ritual and a taste of home.

18. Dragon Fruit

The Fruit That Looks Like a Cartoon and Tastes Like Sorbet

Okay, so dragon fruit was one of those plants we just had to try because... I mean, have you seen it?

It looks like it came from a cartoon. Hot pink skin, wild green flames, and then boom, white or red flesh inside with black seeds.

And if you are lucky enough to get a red-flesh one? Just know it will stain everything. From your cutting board to your kids' shirts.

Ask me how I know.

The first time we grew it, we had no idea how wild it would get. We stuck a piece in the ground, gave it a trellis, and next thing you know, it was climbing like it was training for the Olympics.

One night, we walked outside and caught the flowers blooming. And y'all, I gasped.

They only bloom at night. Giant, fragrant, absolutely magical.

But you gotta be quick. By sunrise, they are gone.

18. Dragon Fruit

We have learned that to get fruit, you need two varieties unless it is self-pollinating. And if you want fruit faster, skip the seed and grab a cutting.

Figure 22 Dragon fruit flower

What It Tastes Like

Mild, slightly sweet, and super refreshing. Almost like a sorbet.

The red-flesh ones have more flavor and are sweeter. White-flesh is milder.

18. Dragon Fruit

Texture is like a mix between kiwi and pear. Soft, juicy, with tiny crunchy seeds.

When to Plant

Spring through early summer.

Protect new plants from frost. Or plant in containers you can move indoors when temps drop.

How to Plant

Start from a cutting for faster fruit. Seeds take years. I am talking 5 to 7 years. A cutting will fruit in 1 to 2 years.

Needs a strong trellis or post. Dragon fruit climbs and gets heavy. The cactus arms will sprawl everywhere if you do not give them something to lean on.

Full sun. Well-draining soil. Dragon fruit is a cactus. It does not like to sit in water. Water deeply but let it dry out between waterings. Do not overwater. This is a desert plant that somehow ended up in the tropics.

Prune to shape and encourage flowering. Too many branches means less energy for fruit.

What Can Go Wrong

Mealybugs and ants can damage buds and fruit. Use neem oil or insecticidal soap.

Avoid overhead watering. It can cause stem rot. Water at the base.

If it does not flower, it might not be getting enough sun or the branches might be too crowded. Prune and give it more light.

When to Harvest

The flowers bloom at night. You may need to hand-pollinate with a brush if you do not have two varieties or if pollinators are not visiting.

Self-pollinating types exist, but many need a partner. Plant two different varieties to guarantee fruit.

The fruit is ready when the skin turns from green to bright pink or yellow (depending on variety) and the green flames start to wilt. It should feel slightly soft when you press it.

Do not pick it too early. It will not ripen off the plant.

The Night-Blooming Magic

The flowers are called "moonflowers" and they only bloom for one night.

Giant, white, fragrant. They open at dusk and close by sunrise.

If you catch them blooming, it feels like witnessing something secret. Something rare.

The Fruit and the Pads

Fruit: High in fiber. Great for digestion. Loaded with antioxidants like betalains (especially the red variety). Good source of vitamin C, iron, and magnesium. Low in sugar and calories. A hydrating snack.

Pads (called cladodes): Can be eaten like nopales (cooked cactus) if harvested young. Contain anti-inflammatory compounds. Traditionally used to support blood sugar control in some cultures.

In the Kitchen

Chill it in the fridge before eating. It is best cold.

Cut it in half and scoop it out with a spoon like ice cream.

Blend with frozen bananas or coconut water for a smoothie.

Makes gorgeous juice, popsicles, or fruit salads.

And a warning: eating too much red dragon fruit? Your poop might turn pink. Do not panic. It is harmless.

18. Dragon Fruit

Did You Know?

Dragon fruit comes from a climbing cactus native to Central America.

In Vietnam, it is called "thanh long," meaning green dragon.

19. Pineapple

If You've Never Had a Homegrown Pineapple...

Let me tell you something. If you have never had a freshly grown pineapple, you have never had a pineapple.

I am serious.

It is like biting into a tropical vacation. Sweet, juicy, refreshing. Like sunshine in fruit form.

I do not even know how else to describe it. Just trust me.

Believe it or not, pineapples were actually one of the first things we had in the ground. But we did not even know it.

When we moved in, there was this spiky little thing poking out of the dirt. I was like, "What is this? Some type of cactus?"

We were this close to pulling it out.

Thankfully, my cousin came over and said, "Oh cool, you are growing pineapples."

I said, "We are?"

And just like that, pineapple preservation mission activated.

19. Pineapple

Then my dad came over and saw I had moved it.

And he hit me with the reality check: "You just added two more years."

TWO. YEARS.

Apparently, pineapples are picky. You disturb them, and they start the clock all over again.

So yeah, we had our first pineapple plant just sitting there. Cold, slow, and quiet. We gave up hope.

But then, a few months later, boom. Out popped another pineapple, faster than we expected.

That is when I learned: when pineapples pop, they pop.

Now? We have at least 100 pineapple tops in the ground. I am not playing. And they are doing their thing.

What It Tastes Like

Juicy. Sweet. Sharp. Tangy.

Like the flavor of canned pineapple, but 100 times better. No comparison.

It is softer, not stringy, and the core is even edible when fresh.

You bite into a homegrown pineapple and you understand why people used to consider them luxury fruit.

When to Plant

Anytime it is warm. Spring through fall is ideal. Just keep them warm year-round.

In Florida, you can plant pineapples almost any time. They just need warmth and sun.

How to Plant

Chop off the leafy top of a pineapple. Let it dry for 2 to 3 days. This helps prevent rot.

19. Pineapple

Stick it in well-draining soil. Do not bury it deep. Just enough to keep it upright.

Pineapples grow well in pots or in-ground.

They need sun, warmth, and patience. Lots of patience.

Water when the soil dries out. Overwatering will rot the roots.

Keep weeds and grass away from the base. Pineapples are low growers. If weeds take over, they will smother the plant.

What They Need

Full sun. At least 6 to 8 hours daily.

Sandy, well-draining soil with pH 4.5 to 6.5. Mix in compost for nutrients. But do not use heavy clay or soil that holds water.

Water when dry. Do not keep the soil constantly wet. Pineapples are drought-tolerant once established.

Protect from cold. Temperatures below 50°F can stunt growth. If you are in a colder part of Florida, grow them in containers and bring them in during cold snaps.

What Can Go Wrong

Mealybugs and scale are common. Rinse with water or treat with neem oil.

Avoid overwatering to prevent root rot. This is the number one killer of pineapples.

Cold can stunt growth. Protect in winter or grow in containers if needed.

And if you move them? You just added time to the clock. My dad was right. Do not disturb them once they are planted.

When to Harvest

Eighteen to twenty-four months to fruit. Longer if moved. That is a long time. I know.

Once it fruits, the mother plant dies. But pups (babies) pop up all around it. Those pups become your next generation of pineapples.

The more tops you plant, the more you will have rolling harvests. That is why we have 100 in the ground now. Stagger your planting and you will have pineapples year-round.

You will know it is ready when the pineapple turns from green to golden yellow and smells sweet. The leaves at the top will also start to brown slightly.

Twist it off or cut it at the base. Do not yank. Let it release naturally.

The Fruit and the Core

Fruit: Loaded with vitamin C. Immune booster and skin supporter. Contains bromelain, a natural enzyme that helps with digestion and inflammation. Naturally hydrating and great for summer days. May help with sinus pressure or swelling.

Core: That firm center? Do not toss it. It is packed with bromelain. Helps tenderize meat naturally if you blend or mash it. Can be frozen and added to smoothies.

19. Pineapple

In the Kitchen: Pineapple Fried Rice (Florida-Style)

This is one of those meals that looks fancy but comes together fast, especially if you have got garden pineapple or leftover rice. It is sweet, salty, and a little spicy all at once. The kind of dish that makes the kitchen smell like summer.

You will need:

- 2 cups cooked rice (day-old rice works best)
- 1 cup chopped pineapple (fresh is best, but canned works too)
- 1 cup cooked chicken, shrimp, or tofu (optional)
- 2 eggs, lightly beaten
- ½ cup diced bell peppers
- ½ cup chopped carrots
- ¼ cup green onions or chives
- 2 tablespoons soy sauce
- 1 tablespoon oyster sauce or coconut aminos
- 1 teaspoon curry powder (optional, but adds color and warmth)
- 2 cloves garlic, minced

19. Pineapple

- 1 tablespoon oil for cooking
- Salt and pepper to taste

How to make it:

1. Heat a large pan or wok over medium-high heat with oil. Add the garlic and cook until fragrant.
2. Add your carrots and peppers. Sauté until they start to soften.
3. Push the veggies to one side and pour in the eggs. Scramble them gently, then mix everything together.
4. Add the rice and break up any clumps. Stir-fry for a few minutes so the rice picks up all the flavor.
5. Toss in pineapple, soy sauce, oyster sauce, and curry powder if using. Mix well until everything looks golden and glossy.
6. Add your cooked protein (if using) and green onions. Season with salt and pepper to taste.

Serve hot, right from the pan. Garnish with extra pineapple or a squeeze of lime for a bright finish.

Toni's Tip

Use leftover jasmine or basmati rice. It fries better and will not turn mushy. I like to add a handful of fresh basil or a spoon of epis right at the end for that extra island flavor.

20. Star Fruit

The Fruit That Literally Stars in the Garden

Okay, I am not going to lie. I picked this one because of the way it looked. I mean, star fruit? The name alone makes you feel fancy. When it is sliced, it literally looks like a star. How could I not? But the taste caught me off guard. The first time I bit into one, I did not know what to expect. It was juicy, crisp, and kind of citrusy. Like if an apple, a grape, and a lemon went on a group date. My kids were obsessed with the shape. My husband started using it in his smoothies like he was hosting a health food segment. We ended up planting it because I bought one too many at the store and figured, hey, why not try growing our own? Now it is one of those trees that just keeps producing. And when it is in season? It is giving superstar.

Getting it in the ground

Spring through early fall is your window. Star fruit loves warmth, so if you are in a spot that gets cold, you might want to grow this in a container so you can bring it indoors when the temperatures drop below 50 degrees. It wants full sun, at least six to eight hours a day, and soil that drains well. If you have heavy soil that stays soggy, the roots will rot on you. Mix in some good organic matter before you plant, and keep the base mulched so the roots stay cool without being waterlogged. If you go the container route, use a big one—at least 20 to 25 gallons—to give the roots enough room to stretch out.

Keeping it happy and productive

This tree is pretty low maintenance, but it does like a bit of attention when it is young. Water it regularly while it is establishing itself. Once it is a bit older, it can handle a little drought, but if you want big, juicy fruit, consistent water is the secret. Do not go crazy with the pruning. Star fruit does not need heavy hacking; just trim it lightly to keep it tidy and make sure air can move through the branches. That airflow is key for keeping pests like aphids and scale away. If you see fruit flies hanging around, you can bag the young fruit to keep them safe, but mostly, just let the tree do its thing.

The harvest routine

Star fruit is a rolling producer. You are not going to get one massive haul and be done; you will have waves of fruit throughout the year. Harvest when the fruit is fully yellow with a slight orange hue. The fruit does not ripen much once you pick it, so if you take it while it is still green, it is going to stay tart. If you see a little bruising, do not stress, it is perfectly normal. Just cut around the soft spot and enjoy the rest. Plus, when the tree blooms, you are going to have bees and butterflies everywhere. It is a good sign that your garden is healthy.

A quick word of caution

There is one thing you need to know before you plant this. If you or anyone in your house has kidney issues, you need to skip this fruit. Star fruit is naturally high in oxalates, which can be serious for anyone with kidney problems. Always check with your doctor if you are not sure.

21. Barbados Cherry

The Fruit You'll Fight Birds For

If you want a plant that produces more food than almost anything else in a Florida garden, you want a Barbados cherry. It is a constant producer, but it comes with a catch: you are not the only one watching it. The Barbados cherry, also called Acerola, is a tropical powerhouse. The fruit is tart, sweet, and bright, tasting like a mix between a sour cherry and tropical punch. For a family of six, it is a dream because it is absolutely packed with Vitamin C. My kids eat them like candy, and even though we try to save some for dehydrating or smoothies, they usually get eaten right there in the garden before we even make it back to the house.

The bird battle

Let's be real about the birds. In Central Florida, the cardinals and mockingbirds treat this tree like an all-you-can-eat buffet. I have walked out to the garden, reached for a ripe cherry, and had a bird snatch it right off the branch before I could get my hand there. I have tried the fake owls and the netting. Most of the time, the birds just figure it out. The only way to win is to be faster. I do daily patrols every single morning. If the cherry is bright red and soft, pick it immediately. If you wait until the afternoon, it will be gone.

21. Barbados Cherry

How to get it growing

This is a tropical plant, which means it thrives in our Florida heat. It needs full sun, at least six to eight hours a day. The more sun it gets, the more fruit it will give you. It likes well-draining soil, so while our sandy Florida dirt is okay, I always mix in some good compost to give it a head start. It does not like to sit in wet feet, so do not overwater it to the point of swampiness. If you have a small yard, this tree does great in a large pot. That is actually a big advantage, because this tree has one major weakness: the cold.

A warning on cold snaps

I am speaking from experience here: the Barbados cherry does not handle freezes. You might get away with a single day in the 30s, but anything deeper or longer? It is over. I lost a beautiful four-year-old tree exactly this way. One bad cold snap was all it took to kill a tree I had spent years tending. If your tree is in the ground, you have to be aggressive with protection. Use heavy frost blankets and be ready to move. If it is in a pot, drag it into the garage the second the forecast looks risky. Do not try to tough it out. If you do not protect it, you will be replacing it.

The insurance policy

Because I learned the hard way about cold snaps, I always keep a few backup plants going. Propagating Barbados cherry is surprisingly easy from cuttings. Just take a six inch cutting in the spring, dip it in a little rooting hormone, and keep it in a pot in a protected spot. By the time winter rolls around, you will have a young, backup tree that you can easily move inside if a freeze is coming. It is the best insurance policy you can have in the garden.

Keeping it tidy

This tree grows fast. You can let it go and it will become a large, messy shrub, or you can prune it into a clean, single-trunk tree shape. I prefer to keep mine pruned to about six or eight feet. It makes it easier to harvest and much easier to cover when those random freezes hit. I usually do a light pruning after a big harvest wave to keep the shape in check. Unlike some fruit trees that give you one big harvest a year, the Barbados cherry fruits in waves. You will get a burst of flowers, then cherries, then a short break, then it starts all over again.

Toni's Tip

Don't pick them when they are orange, or they will be way too sour. Wait until they are deep red and have a little give when you squeeze them. That is when the sugar content is highest. Just remember, the birds are looking for that same red color. This tree is a workhorse. It is compact, it is fast-growing, and it feeds the family all year long. Just respect the cold, keep those backups growing, and be prepared to do a little hand to beak combat to get your share.

22. Lychee

The Sweet Fruit That Makes You Feel Fancy

I used to think lychee was just something you ordered in a bubble tea or saw at a fancy market, the kind of place where everything looks too pretty to touch. But then my husband, Jermaine, said, "We should grow one." I blinked twice. "You mean that juicy grape-looking thing with the bumpy skin?"

Yep. That one.

Now, let me tell you, this tree is high-maintenance. It wants the right weather, the right humidity, and the right amount of chill hours, but not too much chill. Basically, it wants to be pampered. But when it's happy, it delivers like royalty. The fruit is delicate, floral, and juicy. It's the kind of harvest that makes you stop and ask, "Why have I not been growing this all my life?"

What It Tastes Like

The fruit is juicy and sweet with a slightly floral finish, almost like a tropical grape with a hint of rose. The texture inside is smooth and jelly-like. Just remember: do not eat the seed. Pop the flesh out, enjoy the juice, and discard the rest.

The Practical Realities of Planting

Lychees are native to China and have been grown as a delicacy for thousands of years, but they can be tricky in Florida. They need a tropical to subtropical climate (Zones 9b–11) and full sun.

- **Soil Needs:** Lychee needs well-draining, slightly acidic soil (pH 5.0 to 6.5). Sandy loam enriched with compost works best. Avoid high-lime soils, as they can cause nutrient lockout where the tree just stops taking in what it needs.
- In Florida, I recommend planting on a mound or a raised bed. Our heavy rains can drown the roots, and lychee will not tolerate sitting in water.
- Water regularly while the tree is young. Once it's mature, you can let the soil dry out a bit between waterings.

Hard Truth: The "Chill" Paradox

This is the secret no one tells you: Lychee needs cool winter temperatures—not freezing, just cool—to trigger fruiting. This makes them very tricky in certain parts of Florida. If it's too warm, you get beautiful green leaves but zero fruit. If it's too cold, the tree is gone.

Here are the varieties that tend to hold their own in our neck of the woods:

The "Must-Haves" for Central Florida

- Mauritius: If I had to pick one for a beginner, this is it. It is widely considered the most reliable producer in Florida. It is more cold-tolerant than other varieties, and it consistently produces a heavy crop of sweet, juicy fruit. If you want the best chance of actually harvesting something instead of just looking at pretty leaves, start here.
- Brewster: This is the classic Florida lychee. It is a vigorous grower and produces a really high-quality, delicious fruit. The trade-off? It can be a little more sensitive to weather swings than the Mauritius, but it is a proven performer in our climate.
- Sweetheart: This one is a bit of a fan favorite because it has smaller seeds and really excellent, consistent fruit quality. It is known for being a bit more compact and manageable than the massive Brewster trees, which is a huge win if you have a smaller backyard.

A few things to keep in mind

When you go to the nursery, do not let them talk you into a seedling. You want a grafted tree, every single time. A seedling is a decade-long wait that usually ends in disappointment, while a grafted tree is already primed to give you fruit in a few years.

Also, look for the most reputable nursery in your area. You want a tree that has been acclimated to our Florida humidity and heat from the start.

Toni's Tip

Lychees hate sitting in water. Do not just dig a hole in the dirt and drop it in. I always recommend planting your lychee on a mound. Build up a gentle slope of high-quality soil so that the roots are slightly elevated. This ensures that when we get those heavy afternoon summer thunderstorms, the water drains away from the trunk instead of sitting there and rotting your roots. It is the best way to give them that "well-drained" life they crave.

Pests and Prevention

You aren't the only one who thinks this fruit is fancy. You'll have to watch out for:

- **Mites and Scale:** Use sulfur spray for erinose mites and neem oil for scale or aphids.
- **The Big Eaters:** Fruit bats and birds will clear a tree in one night. Use tree netting as the fruit starts to ripen or you won't get a single bite.
- **Airflow:** Prune the tree to keep air moving through the branches. This helps prevent Anthracnose and root rot.

In the Kitchen

We usually eat them fresh right off the tree, just peel and pop. If you manage to get enough into the house, they are incredible in fruit salads, cocktails, or even homemade sorbet. They make a great fancy drink moment when added to iced tea or sparkling water.

23. Bananas and Plantains

23. Bananas and Plantains

The Backyard Takeover You Asked For (Kinda)

You cannot say you are from Florida and not have bananas or plantains somewhere in your yard. Drive through any Caribbean neighborhood in Miami and you will see them — hanging over fences, crowding the corners of yards, shading out whatever was growing next to them. They belong here. And once you plant one, Florida will make sure you always have them.

When we moved into our house, there were already bananas in the backyard. For three years they just sat there being beautiful. Big, glossy leaves, dramatic height — the whole production. No fruit. I fed them. I waited. I started to think they were ornamental. Then one morning I looked out and there it was: a full hand of bananas bending a stalk I had stopped paying attention to. And then they did not stop.

That first harvest turned into a banana explosion. We were giving bags away to neighbors. We were freezing them. We were eating bananas with everything. We learned fast that if you plant bananas, you are committing to bananas. They send out underground shoots — rhizomes — like tiny rebels. Every week a new pup shows up next to the main plant, ready to take over whatever space you give it. We finally stopped fighting it and created what we now call Banana Alley: a whole dedicated section of the yard for our Apple bananas, Ice Cream bananas, and plantains. We gave them their territory and they gave us fruit all year. That is the deal.

Why Plantains Are Personal

My husband Jermaine moved to Miami from Ohio. He will tell you the reason he stayed was the plantains. Rice, beans, and a side of maduros — he was done. He had been vegan for ten years by then, and plantains were his anchor food. Filling, satisfying, something he could eat at every meal without ever getting tired of them. I understood that completely, because in my family, plantains were never a side dish. They were the requirement. You could have the most elaborate plate of food, but if there were no plantains, something was missing.

Growing up Haitian, we had our own plantain traditions alongside the Caribbean ones. Fried sweet plantains with griot — crispy pork marinated in sour orange and herbs — is one of the foods I associate most with home. The sweetness of the maduro against the acid of the griot, that combination is comfort food on a level that is hard to explain unless you grew up eating it. We planted plantains in this yard because we needed them. Not because it seemed like a good idea.

Now we have five plantain plants. That felt like a lot until we realized how fast a household goes through them.

What They Need

Bananas are not trees, they are giant herbs, which surprises people every time. And like any herb that grows to fifteen feet tall, they are hungry and thirsty. Pick the sunniest spot you have, somewhere sheltered from the wind if you can manage it. Those big leaves look sturdy but they tear easily, and a heavy wind can knock a whole stalk over right before the fruit is ready. I have lost a harvest that way. It only happens once before you start thinking about wind protection.

The soil needs to drain well but stay consistently moist. I work in compost before planting and mulch heavily around the base, it holds moisture and keeps the roots from baking in the summer heat. Bananas in Florida do not need complicated irrigation. They need you to notice when it has been dry for two weeks and give them a long, deep soak. They will tell you when they are thirsty. The leaves start looking dull before they droop.

Listen, bananas do not respect boundaries. Give each clump at least five to eight feet from the next one, or you will have a wild jungle taking over your yard faster than you think. The underground rhizomes spread no matter what, so plan your "Banana Alley" before you plant, not after.

But the real secret to keeping them healthy and producing is a rule called the Grandfather, the Father, and the Son. You never want a massive, overcrowded clump fighting for nutrients. You only want three generations growing at one time: the main tall stalk making fruit right now (the Grandfather), the half-grown stalk getting ready for next season (the Father), and the tiny pup just poking out of the soil (the Son).

And here is the thing nobody warns you about: each stalk produces exactly one bunch of fruit in its entire lifetime. When you harvest it, you have to cut that main stalk all the way down to the ground.

Let me tell you, it feels completely wrong the first time. You—or in my case, Jermaine with a handsaw—are chopping down a massive plant that took up to two years to finally fruit. It feels like throwing away all that hard work. But those pups, those side shoots at the base, are already waiting. One of them steps up to become the next producing stalk. The plant keeps going. You just have to trust the cycle.

As for which variety to choose: if your yard is small, the Dwarf Namwah is your friend — shorter plant, sweet fruit, manageable footprint. If you want something that can handle a cold snap (and Florida does throw them), the Ice Cream banana, also called Blue Java, is cold-tolerant and has a flavor that earns the name. The Apple banana, or Manzano, is my personal favorite for eating fresh — small, sweet, with a slight tang that supermarket bananas do not have. And for cooking, a Dwarf Puerto Rican plantain is what you want. It fries beautifully, stays firm when green, and gets deeply sweet when fully ripe.

The Underground Rebels

The biggest mistake I see people make is planting bananas right next to a fence, a foundation, or a garden bed they actually care about. Those rhizomes do not respect property lines. They will travel under concrete if you let them. If you do not stay on top of digging out the pups, and I mean consistently, every month — they will take over in a way that is genuinely difficult to reverse. Plant them where they can spread. Name the zone. Own it. Then let them do what they do.

In the Kitchen: Two Traditions, One Fruit

In this house, plantains serve two masters. There is the Caribbean side — the tostones, the maduros, the thing that has to be on every plate — and there is the Haitian side, where fried sweet plantain sits next to griot and pikliz at every family gathering that matters.

For tostones, you want green plantains — firm, starchy, not a yellow spot on them. Peel them and slice about an inch thick. Fry in oil over medium heat until golden on both sides, then pull them out and smash each one flat with the bottom of a glass or a tostonera if you have one. Back into the hot oil for the second fry — that is where the crunch comes from. Salt them immediately while they are hot. They should be crisp on the outside and soft in the middle, and they will disappear off the plate before you finish making the rest of dinner.

For maduros, you have to wait. The skin needs to be fully yellow, spotted black, almost past what looks edible to someone who has never cooked them. That is peak sugar. Peel them, slice on a diagonal, and fry in a little oil until deep golden brown and caramelized on the edges. The smell is something else. My kids come running from across the house when they hear that sizzle.

And then there is griot night. When I make the Haitian griot — pork marinated in sour orange and herbs, fried until crispy — maduros are non-negotiable. The sweetness cuts through the richness of the pork in a way that makes everything better. My mother made it that way. Her mother made it that way. We grow the plantains so we can keep making it that way.

Toni's Takeaway: Bananas and plantains are not just plants. They are production, they are culture, and they are the kind of abundance that reminds you why you started a garden in the first place. Give them their space, respect the underground rebels, and be ready — because once they start, they do not stop.

Banana or Plantain? Here's How to Tell

By the fruit: Plantains are larger, thicker-skinned, and stay starchy even when ripe. Cut one open raw and it is firm and almost white, like a potato — that is a plantain. Bananas are smaller, thin-skinned, and turn sweet as they yellow.

By the plant: Plantain plants tend to grow taller with wider leaves. The pseudostem — the thick trunk-like stalk — often has a reddish or purplish tinge at the base. Banana plants are usually green all the way up.

By the bunch: When fruiting, plantain fingers are blockier and more angular. Banana fingers are rounder and more curved, and the whole bunch hangs lighter.

The honest truth: When they are young plants just growing in the yard, they look almost identical. The real difference shows up once they fruit. Know what you planted, or wait and see what comes in.

24. Katuk

The Supergreen Nobody Talks About (But Should)

My toddlers figured out Katuk before I did. They would walk past it in the yard, pull a leaf, and just eat it. No cooking, no dressing, no asking me if it was okay. Just straight from the bush, like they were in a cartoon. I watched that happen a few times before I thought, wait - maybe I should actually pay attention to this plant.

We had planted it after reading about high-protein leafy greens that could survive a Florida summer. Most leafy greens give up by June. They bolt, they burn, they turn bitter and tough. Katuk did none of that. It just kept growing. And the more we cut it, the more it gave back. Low maintenance, high return - exactly how we like things in this garden.

The Summer Survivalist

In Florida, we are used to the garden looking a little sad in the middle of July. You walk out there and your kale is crispy, your lettuce has bolted, and even the weeds look like they are struggling. That is when Katuk really shines. While everything else is giving up, Katuk is lush, green, and producing some of the most nutrient dense leaves you can find.

24. Katuk

I call it a sneaky green because it does not have that bitter, medicinal taste that a lot of health foods have. If you have never had it, the young leaves taste remarkably like raw peas. They are sweet and nutty. The older leaves are still edible, but they get a bit tougher, so they are better when you cook them down. You can add the young ones raw to a salad or sauté them just like you would with spinach.

Why It Is a Nutritional Powerhouse

Katuk is a powerhouse that does not get enough credit. For a leafy plant, it is incredibly high in protein, reaching up to 49 percent protein in dry weight. It is also rich in vitamins A, B, and C along with calcium and iron. In Southeast Asian cultures, it is known for boosting energy and supporting lactation, which makes it a great addition for busy moms. Even the young shoots are edible and packed with nutrients. We often harvest the top few inches of a growing stem and use it just like asparagus.

Bringing Katuk Home

If you are looking to add this to your garden, you do not necessarily need to go out and buy a big, expensive pot. One of the best things about Katuk is how easy it is to grow from a cutting. If you have a friend with a bush, just ask for a few six inch pieces of a semi woody stem. Stick those directly into some warm, moist soil, and they will usually start taking root before you even have time to worry about them.

When you are picking a spot, look for somewhere with partial shade. While it can handle the full Florida sun once it is established, it really thrives when it has a little protection from the afternoon heat. Just make sure the soil stays moist and you have a good layer of mulch down to keep those roots cool. Once it starts reaching for the sky, do not be afraid to head back out there with your shears. Keeping it trimmed to about waist height makes it much easier to harvest those pea flavored leaves for your morning smoothie.

The Edible Privacy Fence

24. Katuk

Because Katuk grows so fast and stays so green, it makes for a fantastic edible hedge. If you plant them a few feet apart, they will fill in and create a beautiful privacy screen that you can actually eat. We have found that the more we harvest, the bushier the plant becomes, so do not be shy with the pruners. It is one of the few plants in the garden that actually rewards you for being a little aggressive.

Figure 23 Our Katuk from a cutting

Another plus is that it tends to attract beneficial bugs while deer usually leave it alone. It is easy to overlook at big garden centers, so you might have to ask around or get a cutting from a fellow gardener to get started. I found one lonely plant at our local Lowes. You can also grow Katuk in pots if you give it enough room, so aim for at least a five to seven gallon container.

In the Kitchen

The easiest thing we do with Katuk is throw it in the morning smoothie. It blends completely smooth and barely changes the flavor - which matters when you are trying to get greens into kids who are watching you closely. That is the version my toddlers get. They have no idea.

For dinner, I sauté the leaves with garlic and a little sesame oil, same as you would spinach. It stays firm enough to hold up in soups and stews if you add it at the end. And the citrus salad - young Katuk leaves, a squeeze of orange or lime, some fresh fruit alongside it - that one my kids actually ask for. Which, if you have kids, you know is the highest compliment a vegetable can receive.

25. Leaf of Life

The One That Comes Back No Matter What

This plant right here has a special story because it came straight from my dad. He did not give me a pot or a tag with a name on it. He just handed us a raw clipping and said five words: "Put it in the ground."

That was it. If you know my dad, you know that is all you need to hear. There were no instructions, no explanation of what it was, and no advice on how to water it. It was just a matter of trust. So we did exactly what he said. We dug a little hole in the corner of the yard, stuck the stem in the dirt, and walked away. We honestly forgot about it for a while.

Fast forward a bit, and my cousin came over to visit. We were walking through the garden, looking at the peppers and the tomatoes, when she stopped dead in her tracks. She pointed at that patch of green my dad had started and looked at me like I was crazy.

"Wait, hold on," she said. "Cuz, do you know what you are growing right there?"

I just shrugged. "Yeah, my dad told me to plant it."

She shook her head. "Girl, that is the Leaf of Life. That is the Miracle Leaf. Do you even know what that thing does?"

I had no clue. I was just watering it because my dad said so. She started rattling off the benefits. She talked about lung support, immune support, fighting inflammation, and how the old folks used it for asthma and chest colds. I ran straight to the internet to fact check her, and sure enough, she was right. This plant is loaded with healing power. And here I was, just letting it do its thing in the background.

The Plant That Refuses to Quit

The wildest part about the Leaf of Life is that it is practically immortal. It earned its name. Every time I forget about it or think it is finally gone after a rough season or a dry spell, boom, it comes back. It pops up like nothing ever happened.

It does not matter how much sun it gets or how little water I give it. It does not care how wild the Florida weather has been. It is like the plant knows its purpose is to survive, so it refuses to quit. I have a lot of respect for that kind of resilience. It is not the showiest plant in the garden. It does not have big, beautiful flowers that make you stop and stare. But it is always there when you need it.

The Magic Trick of Growing It

If you want to feel like a magician in the garden, grow this plant. It is scientifically known as *Kalanchoe pinnata*, but the way it grows feels like magic. You do not even need a seed.

25. Leaf of Life

/

If a single leaf falls off the plant and lands on the soil, tiny baby plants will start growing right out of the scalloped edges of that leaf. You will walk out one morning and see a ring of tiny babies outlining the mother leaf. Because of this, it self propagates easily. If you leave it alone, it will spread.

It prefers well drained soil and full sun, but honestly, it will grow in partial shade too. It is extremely drought tolerant because it stores water in those thick, succulent leaves. You really only need to water it when the soil is completely bone dry. Just be careful in North Florida because it does not like the cold. If a freeze is coming, bring it inside.

What It Tastes Like

I will be honest with you: nobody is eating this for the flavor. It is mildly tangy and slightly bitter, almost like if aloe vera met a spinach leaf. The leaves are tender and can be eaten raw, blended, or cooked, but you usually want to mix it with something else.

We like to blend a couple of young, fresh leaves with water, lemon juice, and a touch of honey. Once you strain it, you have a light, powerful health drink that feels good going down. You can also steep the fresh or dried leaves into a tea, which pairs really well with ginger if you need something soothing for a sore throat or a cough.

Secrets form the Kitchen

If you are going to blend it, I have one warning for you: wear an apron. The green juice from this plant can stain your clothes, and it does not like to come out.

Also, keep in mind that you do not need a lot. Just one or two leaves in a green smoothie is plenty to get the benefits without overpowering the taste of your fruit. You can also chop a few leaves and toss them into a soup or stew right at the end of cooking, just like you would with spinach or kale.

Toni's Tip:

Most people grow this for healing, not for looks. It is a connection to a tradition of medicine that goes back generations in the Caribbean, Africa, and Asia. It is a symbol of resilience. Even if you think you have a black thumb, trust me on this one. Put it in the ground, walk away, and let it bring a little life to your garden.

26. Zinnias

The Edible Garden's Best Friend (That You Can't Eat)

The summer I planted Zinnias, everything changed. Not the Zinnias themselves - they did exactly what they were supposed to do, bloomed big and bright and asked for almost nothing. What changed was everything around them. The bees came first. Then the butterflies. Then the garden started producing in a way it never had before. The cucumbers that had been struggling set fruit. The squash vines that had been flowering and dropping started holding on. I did not change what I was doing. I just added the flowers.

I know this is a book about food. And Zinnias are not food - you cannot eat them, they are not medicinal, they will not go into your soup. But here is what I have learned about a food garden: you cannot grow food alone. You need the pollinators to show up, and pollinators go where the flowers are. If your yard is all leaves and vegetables with nothing blooming, the bees have no reason to come. And if the bees are not coming, your cucumbers, your melons, your squash, your passionfruit - none of it sets fruit the way it should. Zinnias are the invitation. They bring the help you need to eat.

That is why they are in this book. Not as a decoration. As a strategy.

Built for the Florida Heat

26. Zinnias

One of the things I appreciate most about Zinnias is that they did not make me work for them. Florida summers are brutal, and I have killed more than a few flowers trying to add color to the garden - things that looked beautiful at the nursery and turned to mush by July. Zinnias are native to Mexico. They were made for heat. When everything else is wilting, they are wide open and unbothered.

You do not start them indoors or fuss with trays. Direct sow the seeds right into warm soil and step back. They want full sun - give them the sunniest spot in your yard and they will reward you. Shade makes them leggy and sparse. Sun makes them bushy and relentless. There is not much else to it.

The one thing they cannot handle is poor airflow. Florida humidity will bring powdery mildew onto the leaves if you crowd them too close together or water overhead. Give them space between plants and water at the base, not over the top. The leaves will stay clean and the blooms will keep coming.

How to Get the Most Out of Them

There are two things that will take a decent Zinnia plant and turn it into a bloom machine. The first is pinching. When the plant is young and still small, you pinch off the top set of leaves - the very tip of the main stem. It feels wrong the first time. The plant looks fine, so why cut it? But pinching forces the plant to send energy sideways instead of straight up. It branches out, gets fuller, and ends up giving you three or four times the flowers you would have gotten otherwise.

The second is deadheading[21]. Once a flower fades and starts to dry on the stem, cut it off. When you leave spent flowers on, the plant reads that as mission accomplished - it made a flower, the flower went to seed, the work is done. When you cut the spent flower, the plant tries again. It keeps blooming through the season instead of peaking and stopping. Snip and it gives you more. It is one of those gardening habits that feels tedious until you see the difference.

More Than a Pretty Face

Beyond the pollinators, Zinnias pull another trick: they act as a trap crop. Aphids and certain pests are drawn to Zinnias before they go looking for your vegetables. So the Zinnias take the hit and your kale and peppers stay clean. I started noticing this in my own garden - the Zinnias would occasionally show aphid clusters on the stems, but my food crops right next to them were untouched. The flowers were doing double duty. Attracting the good insects, absorbing the bad ones.

The Gift That Keeps Coming Back

NASA grew Zinnias on the International Space Station - part of an experiment in growing food in zero gravity. I think about that every time I see them just thriving in my backyard in the Florida heat with almost no help from me. If they can grow in space, they can grow anywhere.

---

[21] **Deadheading:** This is just a fancy word for giving your plant a haircut. It means snipping off the dead or fading flowers. When a flower dies, the plant thinks its job is done and puts all its energy into making seeds. If you cut that dead flower off, you trick the plant into putting its energy back into making *more* flowers. It keeps the plant blooming longer and stops it from looking crispy.

26. Zinnias

My favorite thing about them is that you buy them once. At the end of the season, I let the last round of flowers dry out completely on the stalk. Then I crumble the dried heads in my hand over a bag and shake the seeds loose. They are easy to see - little arrow-shaped pieces packed into the center of the dried bloom. I save them in an envelope, labeled with the color and the year, and by the next spring I have more seeds than I know what to do with. Now they come up like confetti across the yard every season. I have not bought Zinnia seeds in years.

Toni's Takeaway: A row of Zinnias near your vegetables can change the whole energy of the garden. They bring the bees, they absorb the pests, they make the yard a place you want to spend time in. And at the end of the season they give you next year's seeds for free. Plant the flower. Your food will thank you.

27. Aloe Vera

The Plant That Heals From the Inside Out (Literally)

Aloe vera is one of those plants my grandma always had. And man, she was the queen of outdoor remedies. Not a scratch went by without her saying, "Go snap a leaf."

If I got a burn from making rice and not following directions? Aloe. If my hair was standing up and doing its own thing? Aloe. She used that one plant for everything, and now that I think about it, she was way ahead of her time. So many of the benefits I know today started right in her yard. Thanks, mamago (my grandma).

What It Tastes Like (Real Talk)

Okay, we have to be honest here. Straight out of the leaf, aloe is slimy, bitter, and tastes a little like regret. You cannot just bite into it like an apple. But if you rinse it well and blend it with citrus, especially pineapple or lime, it becomes a refreshing, slightly tart addition to smoothies or juice. A little goes a long way, though. Do not say I did not warn you.

The Yellow Warning

There is one major rule when it comes to eating aloe. You have to avoid the yellow part of the leaf, which is the latex layer right under the skin. Unless you are trying to clean yourself out fast, you want to rinse that away completely.

Cut a thick leaf, scoop out the clear gel, and rinse it under cold water until all the yellow residue is gone. That clear gel is gold. It supports digestion, gut health, and acts as a natural detox aid without the drama.

27. Aloe Vera

The Pharmacy in a Pot

My grandma knew what she was doing because this plant is a powerhouse. The gel soothes sunburns, cuts, and skin irritation almost instantly. It is anti inflammatory and antimicrobial.

Beyond the skin, it is a game changer for hair. If you have a dry, itchy scalp, using the raw gel as a natural leave in treatment works wonders. It is rich in vitamins A, C, E, and B12. It is basically a beauty routine growing in dirt. Legend has it that even Cleopatra used it in her daily regimen.

How to Grow It

The best part about Aloe vera is that it thrives on neglect. It is a real MVP for anyone who forgets to water their plants. It hates soggy roots, so put it in sandy or cactus style soil and only water it when it is completely dry.

It loves full sun but can handle some shade if that is all you have. You can throw it in a pot or stick it straight in the ground. Just know that it multiplies fast. Tiny baby plants, called pups, will start popping up around the base. You can split one plant into several and gift them to friends, or just let them fill out the pot.

Secrets No One Tells You

You can actually freeze the gel. I like to scoop it out, rinse it, and freeze it into cubes. They are perfect for tossing into a smoothie or rubbing on a sunburn for extra cooling relief.

Also, this plant has a history. It dates back over 6,000 years. The Egyptians called it the plant of immortality, and even NASA studied it for its air purification abilities.

Toni's Takeaway: Whether you are growing it for a burn, a beauty routine, or just to have a plant that forgives you when you forget to water it, Aloe vera belongs in every garden. It is the one plant that takes care of you as much as you take care of it.

28. Wax Apple

The Juiciest Surprise We Ever Grew (And It's Not Even an Apple)

Let me tell you right now, this one fooled me. Wax apple? It sounds like a shiny, fake fruit you would see sitting on a shelf, not something you would actually eat. But oh, was I wrong.

The first time we bit into one, we had to stop and ask, "Wait... what is this?" It is like a pear and a watermelon had a crispy, refreshing baby. No joke. It crunches like a bell pepper, but it is light, juicy, and almost floral.

Here is the kicker: when it is ripe, the birds will fight you for it. There is no warning. One second it is hanging on the tree, and the next it is gone. We have literally stood guard by our wax apple tree. I call it my "giver of all givers" because it produces so much, but only if you can beat the birds to it.

A Flavor Like Nothing Else

The flavor is mild but slightly sweet, with a watery crunch that feels like biting into a chilled fruit puff. Some people say it tastes like rosewater or a floral pear, but honestly, you just have to try it for yourself.

Because of that high water content, it is incredible for hydration. It is low calorie and low sugar, making it a smart snack for balancing blood sugar. In Southeast Asia, it is traditionally used to cool the body down, which is exactly what we need in a Florida summer.

How to Grow It

28. Wax Apple

Despite the name, this is not related to apples at all. It is part of the *Syzygium* family, the same family as rose apples. It loves warm, humid climates and thrives in Zones 9 through 11.

- It loves full sun, but if you are in extreme heat, partial shade is okay. It needs consistent moisture to produce juicy fruit, so do not let it dry out completely.
- **Pots vs. Ground:** It grows well in pots if you keep it moist and protected from the wind.
- **Speed:** One of the best secrets about this tree is that it fruits fast. Sometimes you get fruit in just one or two years from planting.

In the Kitchen

Wax apples are best eaten fresh, chilled, and straight from the tree, if you can beat the wildlife to it. You can slice them into salads or fruit platters for a crunch, or stuff them with cheese for a fancy snack. Just remember that they do not last long after you harvest them. You need to eat them quickly or store them in the fridge immediately.

The Bird Battle Part II

I know I talk about birds a lot, but with the Wax Apple, it is serious. Fruit flies and aphids can be a problem, but the birds are the main competition. Bagging the fruit on the tree helps, or you can try netting. If you are not on guard, you will lose the harvest.

29. Mangoes

The Star of the Backyard

If you grew up in Miami like I did, you already know that a mango tree in the backyard was not a luxury. It was standard. It was just like having grass. Bananas were extra, but mangoes were a must. We had so many growing up that we would make juice, share with the neighbors, and still not be sick of them by the end of the summer.

I honestly thought there were maybe two kinds of mangoes in the world. Then my husband, Jermaine—who is from Ohio, mind you, came in talking about Lemon Zest, M4, Carrie, and more. I was looking at him like, "What in the mango madness is this?"

So of course, we planted one. It flourishes for two years, finally looking ready to fruit, and then BAM. A cold snap came through and knocked that tree down. I cried. I am not even ashamed to say it. I cried over a tree. We lost every single leaf overnight.

But we did not give up. We did the scratch test, where you scratch the bark to check for green underneath, and miraculously, it passed. We gave it some time to bounce back, but we made a decision right then and there. Never again. That tree got a big pot all to itself. No more risking it in the ground. That mango is protected like royalty now.

Picking Your Player

Because we moved to container gardening for our mangoes, we had to get smart about which varieties we chose. Mangoes are rich, sweet, and juicy, but not all of them taste the same. The Carrie is rich and fiberless, while the Lemon Zest gives you that tangy sweet kick. If you are growing in containers like we are now, the Pickering and Nam Doc Mai are the best choices because they stay naturally compact. If you have the space in the ground and want a massive tree, the Valencia Pride is a strong grower.

Regardless of which one you pick, you need to know that these trees hate wet feet. They love full sun and well drained sandy soil. If you are planting in the ground and your drainage is poor, plant it on a mound. If you are in a pot, make sure it drains fast.

The Patience Game

Here is the secret no one tells you about mangoes: if you want fruit fast, you need to buy a grafted tree. A grafted tree can fruit in two to four years, whereas a seedling can take six years or more. And once it starts producing, get ready. A single mature tree can produce up to 300 fruits a year with the right care.

You also have to watch out for the humidity. In Florida, Anthracnose fungus is common, which shows up as black spots on the leaves or fruit. The best way to prevent it is to be brave with your pruning shears. Keep the tree open so air can flow through the branches.

29. Mangoes

Why We Do It

Beyond the taste, mangoes are a powerhouse. They are packed with Vitamin C and A for immunity and skin health. They are loaded with fiber for digestion and antioxidants to fight inflammation. It is natural sugar for energy without being empty calories.

Toni's Takeaway: Mangoes originated in India over 4,000 years ago, but Florida has become home to over 100 varieties thanks to backyard growers like us. Whether you plant it in the ground or pamper it in a pot, growing your own mangoes connects you to a tropical tradition that is worth every bit of effort. Just keep an eye on that thermometer, because even a light freeze can break your heart.

30. Moringa

Figure 24 Moringa after 1 year planted

The Tree That Changed My Mind About Tea

Moringa was not just something we picked up because it sounded good. This one hit home. See, growing up, my dad did not believe in over the counter medicine. I was maybe six or seven years old, and this man believed everything could be fixed with a leaf, a boil, and a cup. He would walk right into the backyard, grab some green thing off a tree, boil it, and say, “Drink this.” No questions asked.

Back then, I was so over it. Every time I got a sniffle or a cough, here came a new tea. One for the belly, one for the head, one for sleep. I did not even know what I was drinking half the time. I just thought, “What is this man doing now?”

Now I am the one walking outside with a baby on my hip, picking leaves for tea just like my daddy did.

The Postpartum Reality Check

30. Moringa

Everything changed for me after having a baby at forty. Postpartum hit me with something new: high blood pressure that just would not go away. No matter what I tried, the pills gave me more side effects than relief. I was dizzy, foggy, and frustrated. That is when I remembered that we had Moringa in the yard.

We had one of the most powerful plants right outside, and I was ignoring it like it was just another tree. I started drinking the tea again every other day. Slowly, my pressure started to level out. I am not saying it is a miracle cure for everyone, but for me, it reminded me why we grow food. It reminded me why we reach for the garden before the cabinet. This plant right here is one of my reasons.

A Powerhouse for Mothers

In parts of Africa and India, Moringa is often called the Miracle Tree or Mother's Best Friend. It is used in global nutrition programs to fight malnutrition because it is one of the few plants that contains complete plant protein with all nine essential amino acids.

For me, it was about the energy boost without the caffeine crash. The leaves are high in iron, calcium, potassium, and magnesium. They support blood sugar balance and are incredible for lactation and hormone health, which is exactly what a new mom needs.

What It Tastes Like and How to Use It

If you eat the fresh leaves raw, they are peppery and earthy, almost like arugula with a kick. You can toss them into sautéed greens, soups, or lentils. We even blend them with olive oil and garlic for a DIY immune boosting pesto.

However, I usually drink it as a tea. The flavor is herbal, clean, and slightly bitter, but it smooths out perfectly if you steep it with lemon balm, ginger, or honey. You can also dry the leaves and grind them into a powder to sprinkle into smoothies or baked goods. It is a simple way to hide a lot of nutrition in a small package.

How to Grow It

Moringa thrives in full sun and hot weather, making it perfect for Zone 9 and up. It grows incredibly fast, shooting up ten to fifteen feet in a single season. Because it grows so fast, the secret is to prune it often. The more you cut, the more it grows, so do not be shy. If you let it flower, leaf production slows down, so keep it trimmed if you are growing it for the greens.

It loves sandy, well drained soil and hates having wet feet. You can start it from a seed or a cutting, and both root easily. It even grows well in pots if you start with at least a seven gallon container and size up as it gets bigger.

Toni's Takeaway: Whether you call it the Miracle Tree or just a backyard pharmacy, Moringa earns its space in the garden. It is drought tolerant, it grows with very little care, and it might just change your mind about tea the way it changed mine. Just remember to harvest in the morning when the nutrients are strongest.

31. Callaloo (Amaranth)

The Taste of Island Comfort

Sunday mornings growing up had a smell. It started early, before anyone was fully awake, and by the time you made it to the kitchen there was always a pot already going. Callaloo, sauteed down with garlic and onion, sometimes coconut milk if it was a good week. That smell is the reason I grow it now. Not because it is the easiest thing in the garden or the most impressive. Because when I walk outside in the morning and smell those leaves in the heat, I am back in that kitchen.

If you have ever eaten Callaloo from a Caribbean home, you know the flavor I am talking about. Deep, earthy, somewhere between spinach and collard greens but heartier than either one. For us, growing it is about keeping that connection right here in the backyard.

Heat is the Secret Ingredient

While most leafy greens wilt and give up the moment the Florida sun starts blazing, Callaloo is just getting started. It thrives in the heat. In fact, the hotter it gets, the more it grows. It is the perfect answer to the summer garden gap when your lettuce and kale have long since bolted.

You want to plant this in the spring or early summer. The trick to keeping it delicious is to harvest the leaves while they are young and tender. If you wait too long, they can get tough, so keep your scissors handy and keep cutting.

In the Kitchen

You can cook this just like spinach, but if you want the real experience, you have to do it right. Sauté the leaves with garlic, onions, and a splash of coconut milk. That coconut milk softens the earthiness and turns a simple side of greens into a rich, creamy dish that tastes like island comfort.

The Circle of Life

The best part about Callaloo is how low maintenance it is. If you let it flower at the end of the season, it will produce seeds that you can save for next year. Or, if you are like me and sometimes let nature take its course, it will often reseed itself. You will look up next spring and see it popping back up, easy as breathing.

Toni's Takeaway: This is the green that loves you back. It feeds you through the hottest days of the year, it reminds you of where you came from, and it asks for almost nothing in return. Every Florida garden needs a patch of Callaloo.

32. Roselle (Florida Cranberry)

The Fall Harvest Florida Actually Gets

Roselle brings fall to Florida. While the rest of the country gets changing leaves and crisp air, we get this tart, bright, and beautiful plant. It is widely known as the Florida Cranberry, and for good reason. It gives us that seasonal shift we crave, even when it is still eighty degrees outside.

The part you harvest is the red calyx that forms after the flower blooms. They look like little jewels in the garden, and they are what you use to make incredible teas, jams, and tangy sauces.

Timing is Everything

You want to start Roselle in late spring once the soil warms up. It loves the heat of summer to grow big and bushy, but the magic happens when the days start getting shorter. By October, you will have baskets full of these red calyxes ready to harvest.

A Flavor Like No Other

The flavor is exactly like hibiscus and cranberry had a Florida baby. It is sour, fruity, and punchy. It makes for perfect homemade drinks or syrups that have that deep red color everyone loves.

32. Roselle (Florida Cranberry)

In the Kitchen

If you have ever had Red Zinger tea or Caribbean Sorrel drink, you know this flavor. We love boiling the fresh calyxes with ginger and sugar for a holiday drink, but don't stop there. You can cook them down into a cranberry-style sauce for Thanksgiving dinner, and no one will even know the difference.

Saving the Future

Here is the trick most people miss. When you peel that red fleshy part off to make your tea, there is a round pod left inside. If you picked the fruit young and tender for eating, the seeds inside that pod are usually white and not ready to plant.

If you want to save seeds for next year, you have to let a few of those pods stay on the bush. Wait until the calyx turns brown and brittle. When you can shake the pod and hear the seeds rattling inside, that is when you know they are ready. Crack them open, dry the dark brown seeds on a paper towel, and store them. You will never have to buy Roselle seeds again.

Do not feel like you have to use it all at once. Dry a big batch of the calyxes and store them in a jar. That way, you can enjoy that tart, refreshing tea all year long, long after the season is over.

33. Okinawa Spinach

The Overachiever of the Garden

Let's talk about the overachiever of the garden. By July, when the Florida sun is disrespecting every other green in the yard and the regular lettuce has completely melted into the dirt, Okinawa Spinach is out there thriving. It honestly looks like a fancy landscaping plant. It has bright green leaves on top and a deep, dramatic purple underneath. You would think it belongs in a decorative pot by the front door, but this is a powerhouse edible. Because my gardening style leans a little toward chaotic, I need plants that do not ask me to babysit them. Give this one partial sun, it loves the heat, but it definitely appreciates a break from that brutal afternoon bake—and trim it often. It actually loves the attention. The more you clip, the bushier it gets.

Getting it started

Okinawa Spinach is ridiculously easy to grow from cuttings. Seriously. Grab a stem, stick it in moist soil, and walk away. It will root faster than you can remember where you planted it. You can get it going anytime it is warm—spring through fall is ideal, but in Florida, you can pretty much plant it year round. Just keep an eye on the thermometer and protect it if we get one of those rare, sharp freezes. If you want to grow it in a pot, it does great in a 5 to 7 gallon container with good drainage. Just remember that it loves to spread, so give it a little room or be ready to trim it back.

Keeping it happy

This plant is nearly indestructible. It prefers partial sun to full shade, especially during those hottest hours of the day. If you put it in full sun, the leaves might scorch, so find it a little protection. It likes its soil moist—Okinawa Spinach does not like to dry out completely, so keep it watered and use mulch to help hold that moisture in. If the soil does dry out and the plant wilts, do not panic. Give it a good drink and it will bounce back quickly. Pests mostly leave it alone, but if you do see aphids, just spray them off with a quick blast of water.

The harvest routine

You can start clipping within a few weeks of planting. Harvest anytime the plant has enough leaves—just snip the top few inches of the stems. The plant will bush out and produce even more. This is one of those rare plants that rewards you for being aggressive with the pruners. The more you harvest, the more it grows.

Why it belongs in your kitchen

It is mild and a little nutty, so it does not fight the other flavors in your dish. On those days when I have exactly five minutes to get a meal together between a corporate meeting and the toddlers turning the living room upside down, this is my go to. I can wilt it into a quick stir-fry, or chop it up fine and scramble it right into the kids' eggs. They do not even question the purple confetti in their breakfast. It is packed with vitamins A and C, calcium, and iron, and those purple undersides are full of anthocyanins, the same antioxidants you find in blueberries.

Toni's Tip

My gardening style is a little chaotic, so I need plants that do not complain. Okinawa Spinach is that plant. It does not need much, and when everything else in the garden has given up in July, this is the one that carries you through. Plant it, trim it often, and enjoy the longevity.

34. Surinam Cherry

The Tiny Pumpkin That Beats You to the Punch

The first time I saw a Surinam cherry, I thought someone was growing miniature pumpkins on a tree. It is about the size of a cherry, but it has these ridges running down the sides that make it look like a tiny pumpkin. Bright red, ridged, sitting there on the branch looking ornamental.

Growing up in Miami, these things grew wild everywhere. You would find them in empty lots, on the side of the road, in people's yards who did not even know what they had. We used to pick them as kids, and if you grabbed the wrong one, still orange instead of deep red, you learned real fast. It puckered your whole mouth like you bit into a lemon.

The trick was waiting for the deep red or purple ones. Those were sweet-tart, tropical, juicy. Like a cherry met a cranberry and decided to vacation in Florida.

And here is the thing: Surinam cherries are not actually cherries. They are not even related to regular cherries. They are in the myrtle family. The name is just because they are small, round, and red. But the flavor? Completely different. And the shape? Those ridges make them unmistakable.

Now we have our own tree. And I have learned that growing Surinam cherries means you are in a race. The birds know when they are ripe. The kids know when they are ripe. And if you do not get out there first thing in the morning, you will find an empty tree and a bunch of very satisfied cardinals.

The tree itself is easygoing. Full sun, minimal fuss. The kind of plant you can mostly ignore and it will still produce. But those little ridged fruits? They do not wait for you.

The Ripe vs. Not-Ripe Lesson

Here is what you need to know: color matters. A lot.

Orange Surinam cherries look tempting. They are bright, they are on the tree, and you think, "That is close enough, right?" Wrong. Orange ones will make your face scrunch up like you just bit into a warhead. Sour, astringent, not fun.

Wait for deep red. Even better, wait for purple. That is when the sweetness comes out. That is when it tastes tropical and juicy instead of like punishment.

And here is the trick my neighbor taught me: chill them first. Put them in the fridge for an hour or two before you eat them. It brings out the sweetness and tones down any lingering bitterness. I do not know the science behind it, but it works. Chilled Surinam cherries taste like candy. Room temperature ones taste... fine. There is a difference.

When to Plant

Spring through early fall. Surinam cherry loves warmth and full sun.

In South Florida, you can plant year-round. In Central and North Florida, wait until after the last frost.

This tree does not like cold. If you get freezes where you are, grow it in a pot so you can bring it inside when temps drop.

How We Grow It

Our Surinam cherry lives in full sun. It wants every bit of light it can get. We planted it in sandy soil with some compost mixed in, watered it deeply for the first few weeks, and then pretty much left it alone. Once it was established, it became one of those plants that just does its thing without asking for much.

We space our trees about 6 to 8 feet apart because they spread. And we mulch around the base to keep the roots cool and hold in moisture, but honestly, once this tree settles in, it is drought-tolerant. It does not need constant attention.

The one thing it does not handle well? Cold. This is a tropical plant. We learned that the hard way our first winter when temps dropped into the 30s and the tree dropped half its leaves overnight. It recovered, but it was not happy. Now if we get a freeze warning, we throw a freeze cloth over it or bring it inside if it is in a pot. Anything below 40°F and it starts to struggle. Below freezing? You might lose it entirely.

If you live somewhere that gets real winter, keep this one in a container. That way you can drag it inside when the temps drop and bring it back out when it warms up.

What It Needs

Full sun. At least 6 to 8 hours daily. The more sun, the more fruit.

Well-draining soil. Surinam cherry does not like wet feet. If the soil stays soggy, the roots will rot.

Minimal water once established. Young trees need regular watering, but mature trees can handle drought.

What Can Go Wrong

Birds will eat the fruit before you do. Net the tree or accept that you are sharing.

Fruit flies can be an issue. Bag the fruit while it is young to protect it.

Cold snaps will damage or kill the tree. Protect it during freezes or grow in a container you can move.

If you pick the fruit too early (when it is still orange), it will be sour. Wait for deep red or purple.

When to Harvest

Surinam cherry fruits multiple times a year in Florida. You will have waves of fruit instead of one big harvest.

Wait until the fruit is deep red or purple. Orange fruit is not ripe. It will make you pucker.

The fruit does not last long once ripe. Pick it and use it within a few days.

And here is the trick: chill it before eating. It brings out the sweetness.

Why It Is Good for You

Surinam cherry is high in vitamin C. Supports immunity and skin health.

Contains antioxidants that help fight inflammation.

Good source of fiber. Supports digestion.

Low in calories. A hydrating, guilt free snack.

In the Kitchen

Eat them fresh. Just pop them in your mouth like candy.

Blend into juice. Strain out the seeds and sweeten to taste.

Turn them into jam. Simmer with sugar and lemon juice until thick.

Add to smoothies, fruit salads, or desserts.

Kids love them. Birds love them. And if you beat both to it, you will love them too.

Did You Know?

Surinam cherry is native to Brazil and is also called Pitanga.

It has been grown in Florida for over a century and is naturalized in some areas. You can find them growing wild in empty lots, on roadsides, and in old yards. That is how common they are here.

35. Mulberry

Pure Summer Magic

I remember the first time I saw our mulberry tree really produce. We had planted it maybe two years before, and it had been growing fast but not fruiting much. Then one summer, it exploded.

I am talking berries everywhere. On the branches, on the ground, on the driveway, on the kids' hands, on their faces, on their shirts. Purple everywhere.

My husband walked outside and said, "Did something happen out here?"

Yeah. The mulberry tree happened.

One tree can feed you, your neighbors, and every bird within a mile. And they will all show up. The cardinals, the mockingbirds, the blue jays. They know when the berries are ripe before you do.

But here is the thing: there are enough for everyone. The tree does not stop. It just keeps producing. Day after day, week after week. You pick a handful in the morning, and by afternoon there are more.

The berries are soft, juicy, and taste like a mix between blackberry and fig. Sweet, a little earthy, with just enough tartness to keep it interesting. We toss them in pancakes, bake them into pies, freeze them for smoothies. My kids eat them straight off the tree until their hands and mouths are stained purple.

And yes, they stain everything. Hands, clothes, faces, driveways, sidewalks. Everything turns purple. But in Florida, that is a badge of honor. If your kids come inside looking like they fought a grape, you know you have got a good mulberry tree.

Why Mulberries Work in Florida

Mulberries grow fast. Faster than almost any other fruit tree. You plant one and within a year or two, it is already taller than you. Within three to four years, it is producing fruit.

They thrive in Florida soil. Sandy, loamy, even clay. They do not care. Just give them sun and water and they will grow.

They start producing early. You do not have to wait five or seven years like you do with some fruit trees. Mulberries fruit fast. And once they start, they do not stop.

They handle heat. They handle humidity. They handle drought once established. Mulberries are tough.

And they produce a lot. I mean a lot. One tree can give you more berries than you know what to do with. Which is why you share with the neighbors. And the birds. And anyone who walks by.

Varieties Worth Growing

Not all mulberries are the same. Some are sweeter. Some produce longer. Some stay smaller.

- **Everbearing** is the workhorse. It fruits for months, not weeks. You will be picking berries from late spring through summer. The fruit is sweet, dark purple, and productive. This is the one most people plant in Florida because it just keeps giving.
- **Thai mulberries** are long and skinny instead of round. They taste sweeter than most varieties and the tree stays more compact. Good for smaller yards. The berries look different—more like little fingers than regular mulberries—but they taste incredible.
- **Illinois Everbearing** is another solid choice. Big, sweet berries and heavy production. It is cold-hardy, so if you are in North Florida and get freezes, this one handles it well.
- **Pakistan** mulberries are huge. I am talking 3 to 4 inches long. They are sweet, juicy, and the tree grows fast. But it gets big. Like really big. So give it space.

We have got an Everbearing in our yard because we wanted fruit all summer long. And it delivers. Every morning from May through August, there are fresh berries waiting.

How We Grow It

Our mulberry tree lives in full sun. It wants all the light it can get. We planted it in regular Florida soil, watered it for the first few months, and then pretty much left it alone.

It does not need much. Water when it is young. Mulch around the base to keep the roots cool. Prune it if it gets too tall or too wide. That is it.

We do not fertilize it. We do not baby it. It just grows.

And it spreads. Mulberry trees can get big if you let them. Ours is probably 20 feet tall and just as wide. We prune it back every year to keep it manageable, but honestly, it does not mind. The more you prune, the bushier it gets.

Here is the best part: mulberries are ridiculously easy to propagate from cuttings. You can take a 6 to 8 inch cutting from a healthy branch, stick it in moist soil, and it will root. That is how we ended up with three mulberry trees when we only planted one. We took cuttings, gave some to neighbors, planted some in different spots in the yard. Now we have mulberries everywhere.

Cold? Mulberries handle it. They are deciduous[22], so they drop their leaves in winter and go dormant. A freeze does not bother them. They come back in spring like nothing happened.

What Can Go Wrong

Mulberries are pretty tough, but they can get bugs. Aphids, scale, and whiteflies like to hang out on the leaves. If you see them, spray the tree down with water first. That usually knocks most of them off.

If they come back, use neem oil. Spray the leaves, especially the undersides where bugs like to hide. Do it in the evening so you do not burn the leaves in the sun.

We have also seen caterpillars on our tree. They munch the leaves but usually do not do enough damage to worry about. The birds take care of most of them.

Other than that? Mulberries do not ask for much. No major diseases. No constant pest problems. They just grow.

The Staining Situation

Let me be clear: mulberries stain everything.

Your hands. Your clothes. Your kids' faces. Your driveway. Your sidewalk. The grass underneath the tree. Everything turns purple.

---

[22] **Deciduous** refers to a plant that sheds its leaves annually, usually in the autumn or when the growing season ends. It is nature's way of conserving energy. Instead of trying to keep its leaves alive through a harsh, dry, or cold season, which takes a massive amount of water and effort, the plant simply lets them go and enters a dormant, resting phase.

35. Mulberry

We have learned to just accept it. Purple hands are part of summer. Purple shirts get thrown in the wash with vinegar. Purple driveways get hosed down. Or not. Sometimes we just let it be.

The birds? They stain too. You will see purple bird droppings all over your car, your patio furniture, your fence. It is what it is.

But honestly, it is worth it. Because the fruit is that good. And the tree is that productive. And the kids are that happy.

If you can handle the staining, you can handle mulberries.

When to Harvest

Mulberries ripen in late spring to early summer. Depending on the variety, you might get fruit from April through June.

You will know they are ready when they turn dark purple or black and fall off the tree with a gentle touch. If you have to pull, they are not ready yet.

The best way to harvest? Lay a tarp or sheet under the tree and shake the branches. The ripe berries will fall. The unripe ones will stay on the tree.

Or just let the kids loose under the tree. They will find them.

We check the tree every morning during peak season. Because the berries do not last long once they are ripe. They soften fast. Use them within a day or two, or freeze them.

In the Kitchen

We toss mulberries in pancakes. We bake them into pies. We freeze them for smoothies.

My kids eat them fresh until they look like they fought a grape.

You can make mulberry jam, mulberry syrup, mulberry ice cream. You can dry them like raisins. You can ferment them into wine if you are into that.

They are sweet enough to eat fresh but tart enough to bake with. They hold up well when frozen. And they blend into smoothies without overpowering the other flavors.

Honestly, the hardest part is getting them from the tree to the kitchen before someone eats them all.

35. Mulberry

Did You Know?

Mulberries have been grown for thousands of years. Silkworms eat mulberry leaves, which is why mulberry trees were so important in ancient China for silk production.

There are different types. Black mulberries are the sweetest. Red mulberries are native to North America. White mulberries are milder and less sweet. But in Florida, most people grow named varieties like Everbearing, Thai, or Pakistan because they produce better fruit and fruit longer.

36. Peaches

The Four Year Wait

We have all been there. You see a peach tree at a store, you get excited, and you stick it in the ground thinking nature will do the rest. Then you spend years staring at a stick that refuses to grow, wondering what you did wrong. It is frustrating, but it is a necessary part of the journey. When you finally pull that tree out and replace it with a variety actually meant to thrive in our specific heat and chill hours, the difference is night and day.

Taking Control

There is nothing quite like biting into a peach that you grew in your own yard. Store-bought fruit is bred for shipping and shelf life, not for that juice-down-your-chin sweetness. When you grow your own, you are the one in charge of the quality. You are deciding what goes into the soil, you are watching the fruit ripen on the branch, and you are the one deciding exactly when it is at the perfect stage of sweetness to pick.

It is the best way to show the kids that fruit does not just appear in a plastic clamshell at the grocery store. It is work, it is patience, and sometimes it is a four-year lesson in buying the right tree, but that first harvest makes it all worth it.

The Chill Hour Problem Nobody Warned You About

Here is what most people do not know when they buy that peach tree at the garden center: peaches need chill hours. That means a certain number of hours each winter where temperatures drop below 45 degrees. Standard peach varieties need 600 to 1,000 of those hours to bloom and set fruit. Florida winters do not give you that. So the tree sits there, confused. It never gets the signal that winter happened. It never blooms properly. And you never get peaches.

That is the stick in the ground situation. Not your fault. Wrong tree.

Figure 25 Our 4 yr old unnamed peach tree

The fix is buying a low-chill variety, one that was specifically bred for climates like ours. These trees only need 100 to 300 chill hours, which Florida can actually deliver, even in the south. When you plant the right variety, the tree knows what to do. It blooms in January or February, the fruit develops through spring, and by April or May you are picking peaches. In Florida. From your own yard. It feels like you broke a rule.

Which Varieties to Look For

The names to know are TropicBeauty, Flordaprince, Flordaking, and UFSun. TropicBeauty is probably the most widely available and one of the most reliable for South Florida - it needs very few chill hours and produces a sweet, full-flavored fruit. Flordaprince is a good early producer and handles the heat well. Flordaking gives you a larger fruit if you are in Central Florida with slightly cooler winters. UFSun was developed by the University of Florida specifically for our conditions and is worth hunting down if you can find it.

36. Peaches

Do not buy a peach tree unless the tag tells you the chill hour requirement. If it just says 'peach tree' with no variety listed, put it back. That information matters more than anything else when it comes to whether you will ever eat from it.

What It Takes

Full sun is non-negotiable. Peaches want at least eight hours of direct light a day. Put them in a shaded spot and you will get a pretty tree with very little fruit. Plant them where they get the most sun your yard has to offer.

Drainage is the other thing they are serious about. Peaches do not want wet feet. If your soil stays soggy after rain, the roots will rot before you ever see a bloom. If you have heavy clay or poor drainage, plant on a slight mound or amend heavily with compost before you go in. Well-drained, slightly sandy soil is where these trees are happiest.

Fertilize in early spring when new growth starts and again after harvest. A balanced fertilizer works fine. Do not overdo it or you will push too much leafy growth at the expense of fruit. And prune every year after harvest, opening up the center of the tree so air can move through. Florida humidity creates fungal problems if the canopy gets too dense. A little pruning goes a long way toward keeping the tree healthy and productive.

The wait between planting and first fruit is real. Expect one to three years before a young tree produces a meaningful harvest. Some people see a little fruit in year two. Some wait until year three or four. It depends on the tree, the variety, and the winter you get. The patience is part of the deal. But once a low-chill peach tree settles in and gets a proper Florida winter, it will fruit for years.

In the Kitchen

A homegrown peach picked at full ripeness is a different fruit from what you buy at the store. The flesh is softer, the juice runs, the sweetness is deeper. The first time you bite into one you grew yourself, you will understand why you waited.

We eat most of ours fresh, straight off the tree, still warm from the sun. That is the real reward and it does not need any help. But when we have more than we can eat in a sitting, we slice them into a simple syrup with a little vanilla and freeze them for smoothies through the summer. Frozen Florida peaches in a July smoothie taste like proof that the work was worth it.

For cooking, a peach cobbler with homegrown fruit is one of those things you make once and cannot stop thinking about. Simple batter, sliced peaches, brown sugar, a little butter. Nothing complicated. The peach does the work. You can also do a quick peach jam if you have a big harvest coming in all at once - it keeps for months and reminds you in January that spring is coming again.

Toni's Tip

The four-year wait is not a failure. It is just the price of planting the wrong tree first. Once you know about chill hours and you put the right variety in the ground, Florida will surprise you. Peaches in April. From your yard. That first bite makes you forget every stick you ever stared at.

37. Elderberry

The Immune-Boosting Powerhouse You Cook, Not Snack

Let me tell you about the plant that saved us during cold and flu season.

Elderberry.

We planted it a few years ago after I got tired of buying elderberry syrup at the store for $20 a bottle. I was like, "We have a whole garden. Why am I buying this?"

So we planted elderberry. And it took off.

37. Elderberry

Figure 26 Harvesting Elderberries

It loves Florida's moist soil. It loves the humidity. It grows fast and produces clusters of tiny dark berries that look like they belong in a fairy tale.

But here is the critical part: you cannot just pop these in your mouth like mulberries or blueberries. Elderberries must be cooked before eating. Raw elderberries will make you sick. I am talking nausea, stomach cramps, the whole deal.

So we cook them. We make elderberry syrup. We make elderberry tea. We add them to jams and baked goods. And every winter, when the kids start sniffling, we pull out the elderberry syrup and it works.

This is not just a pretty plant. This is medicine you can grow in your backyard.

Why Elderberry Works Here

37. Elderberry

Elderberry loves moist soil. In Florida, where we get summer rains and humidity, elderberry thrives.

It grows fast. You plant a cutting or a small plant and within a year or two, it is producing berries.

It handles heat and humidity. While some plants struggle in our summers, elderberry just keeps growing.

And it produces a lot. One plant can give you enough berries to make syrup for the whole year.

How We Grow It

Our elderberry lives in partial sun. It can handle full sun, but it really loves a little afternoon shade. Too much blazing sun can stress it out.

We planted it in a spot that stays moist. Not soggy, but moist. Elderberry does not like to dry out completely.

We mulch heavily around the base to keep the soil cool and retain moisture. And we water it regularly, especially during dry spells.

Elderberry is easy to propagate from cuttings. We took a few pieces from our original plant, stuck them in moist soil, and they rooted. Now we have three elderberry bushes when we started with one.

It is deciduous, so it drops its leaves in winter and goes dormant. A freeze does not bother it. It comes back in spring like nothing happened.

What It Needs

Partial sun to full sun. Elderberry prefers a little afternoon shade, but it can handle full sun if you keep it watered.

Moist soil. Elderberry does not like to dry out. Keep the soil consistently moist, especially during hot months.

Mulch to retain moisture and keep the roots cool.

Regular pruning. Elderberry can get leggy if you do not prune it back. Cut it back in late winter to encourage new growth and more berries.

What Can Go Wrong

37. Elderberry

Aphids love elderberry. If you see them clustering on the new growth, spray them off with water or use neem oil.

If the soil dries out too much, the plant will stress. Keep it watered.

And here is the big one: do not eat raw elderberries. They must be cooked. Raw berries, leaves, stems, and roots contain compounds that can make you sick. Always cook the berries before using them.

When to Harvest

Elderberries ripen in late summer to early fall. You will know they are ready when the clusters turn fully dark purple or black and the berries feel plump.

Do not pick them too early. Green or red berries are not ripe and should not be used.

Cut the entire cluster off the plant with scissors or pruners. Then strip the berries off the stems. The stems are toxic, so do not include them in your syrup or tea.

Use the berries within a few days or freeze them for later.

How to Use Them (Always Cooked)

Making elderberry syrup is my favorite way to keep a bottle of "get well soon" in the fridge all winter. Since you're dealing with raw berries, remember that **cooking is mandatory** to make them safe and palatable.

Here is how I do it in my kitchen:

My Simple Elderberry Syrup Recipe

The Ingredients

Dried Elderberries: About one cup. (If you are using fresh, use two cups.)

Water: Three to four cups.

Aromatics: A cinnamon stick, a few cloves, and a slice of fresh ginger root. These add flavor and extra goodness.

Honey: About one cup of raw, local honey. (Wait until the liquid cools down before adding this so you don't kill the beneficial enzymes in the honey.)

The Process

Simmer: Combine the berries, water, and spices in a pot. Bring it to a boil, then turn the heat down to a low simmer. Let it cook uncovered for about 45 minutes to an hour. You want the liquid to reduce by about half—it should look dark, rich, and concentrated.

Mash: Take a potato masher or a fork and gently crush the berries against the side of the pot to release all that good juice.

Strain: Pour the mixture through a fine-mesh sieve or a cheesecloth into a bowl. Use the back of a spoon to press as much juice as you can out of the berries, then discard the solids.

Sweeten: Let the liquid cool down until it is just warm, not hot. Stir in your honey until it is fully dissolved.

Bottle: Pour your finished syrup into a clean glass jar or bottle. Keep it in the fridge.

The Storage Because this is a natural, homemade product without heavy preservatives, keep it in the refrigerator. It usually stays good for about two months. If you notice any weird changes in smell or color, just toss it and start a new batch.

Why It Is Good for You

Elderberries are packed with antioxidants, especially anthocyanins. These help fight inflammation and support immune function.

They are high in vitamin C. Great for immunity, especially during cold and flu season.

Studies suggest elderberry can shorten the duration of colds and flu. That is why elderberry syrup is so popular.

It supports respiratory health. Elderberry has been used for centuries in traditional medicine for coughs, congestion, and sinus issues.

And it is natural. You are not buying a $20 bottle at the store. You are making it yourself from berries you grew.

Did You Know?

37. Elderberry

Elderberry has been used in traditional medicine for centuries. Native Americans used it for fevers, infections, and skin conditions.

In Europe, elderberry is still widely used for colds, flu, and respiratory issues.

The flowers are also edible and can be used to make elderflower cordial or tea. But the berries are the real powerhouse.

And despite needing to be cooked, elderberries are one of the most productive medicinal plants you can grow in Florida.

38. Jaboticaba

The Tree That Stops Conversations

If you ever want to stop someone mid-sentence, show them a Jaboticaba tree. I am serious. We had a neighbor walk over to ask about borrowing the lawnmower, and she stopped mid-sentence when she saw ours. She just stared at it and asked, "Are those... growing on the trunk?"

Yeah, they are.

Jaboticaba fruit grows right on the trunk and branches like the tree is studded with glossy black marbles. It looks magical, like something out of a fantasy movie or a tree wearing fine jewelry. And the taste matches the look. It is sweet, grape-like, and slightly floral. You bite into it, suck out the pulp, and toss the peel, just like a lychee. The skin is a little tart, but the inside is pure candy.

The payoff of patience

38. Jaboticaba

We planted ours about five years ago. For the first few years, it just grew. Slow and steady. No fruit. Just a pretty tree. I started to wonder if we did something wrong, but my husband kept saying, "Patience. It takes time." Then one day, I walked outside and there they were. Little black marbles all over the trunk. I yelled for the kids, and they ran out thinking something was wrong. Nope. Just fruit growing on the tree trunk like magic.

Now, every time it fruits, people stop and stare. It is a showstopper tree that earns every bit of attention it gets. Jaboticaba is not a fast-fruiting tree. If you plant it from seed, you might wait 8 to 15 years before you see fruit. That is why we bought a small grafted tree. Doing that gets you fruit in 3 to 5 years instead. Once it starts, it fruits mul1``le times a year in waves. You will have a flush in spring, another in summer, and sometimes even in fall. So yes, you wait, but the payoff is worth it.

How we grow it

Our Jaboticaba lives in partial sun. It can handle full sun, but it really thrives with a little afternoon shade. Too much blazing sun can stress it, especially when it is young. We planted it in rich, moist soil because Jaboticaba loves organic matter. We mixed in compost before planting and we mulch heavily around the base to keep the soil cool and moist.

You have to water it regularly. This is not a drought-tolerant tree. It needs consistent moisture, especially during fruiting season. If the soil dries out, the fruit can drop before it ripens. It grows really slow, so do not expect it to shoot up like a mulberry or a papaya. Ours is probably 8 feet tall after five years. You can grow this in a large 25 to 30 gallon pot if you have good drainage, but if you get a cold snap, you must protect it. Anything below 30°F for too long can damage it.

What to watch for

Jaboticaba is pretty low-maintenance, but a few things can trip you up. Aphids and scale can show up, so just spray them off with water or use a little neem oil. The biggest thing is just making sure it doesn't dry out. If you are not seeing fruit after a year or two, that is normal. Give it time. It will fruit when it is ready.

When it comes to harvesting, wait for full black. Green or purple fruit is not ripe yet. The fruit turns glossy black and feels soft when you gently squeeze it. The fruit does not last long once it is ripe, so use it within a few days or it will ferment on the tree. We pick it every morning during fruiting season and eat it fresh or freeze it.

Why it is good for you

Jaboticaba is packed with antioxidants, especially in the skin. Even if you do not eat the skin, you are still getting good nutrients from the pulp. It is high in vitamin C, contains anti-inflammatory compounds, and is low in calories. Plus, it is incredibly hydrating, which is perfect for those hot Florida days.

Did You Know?

Jaboticaba is native to Brazil and has been cultivated there for centuries.

The fruit is also called Brazilian grape tree because of how it tastes and how it grows in clusters.

In Brazil, people make jaboticaba wine, liqueur, and preserves. The fruit is so popular that entire festivals are dedicated to it.

And the wood? It is dense and durable. Traditionally used for making tool handles and posts.

But here in Florida, we grow it for the fruit. And the spectacle. Because nothing stops a conversation like a tree covered in glossy black marbles.

39. Jujube

The Chinese Date That Tastes Like Candy

I had never heard of jujube until my husband brought one home from the Asian market.

He handed me this small, reddish-brown fruit that looked like a date and said, "Try this."

I bit into it. Crisp like an apple, sweet like honey, with a texture somewhere between an apple and a date. I was hooked.

"Can we grow this?"

Turns out, yes. And it is one of the easiest fruit trees you can grow in Florida.

Jujube loves heat. It loves sun. It handles drought like a champ. And once it starts fruiting, it does not stop. You will have more jujubes than you know what to do with.

Fresh jujubes taste like a crisp, sweet apple with honey notes. Dried jujubes taste like dates but chewier. They are incredible either way.

And here is the best part: while every other fruit tree in Florida is struggling with pests and diseases, jujube just sits there producing. No drama. No fuss. Just fruit.

Why Jujube Works in Florida

Jujube loves heat. The hotter it gets, the happier it is. While other trees are wilting in July, jujube is thriving.

It handles drought. Once established, jujube does not need much water. It is one of the most drought-tolerant fruit trees you can grow here.

It has very few pests. No major diseases. No constant spraying. Jujube just grows.

It fruits reliably. Once it starts, you will get jujubes every year. No off years. No guessing.

And it is low-maintenance. Plant it, water it when it is young, then mostly leave it alone. It does not ask for much.

How We Grow It

Our jujube lives in full sun. It wants every bit of light it can get.

We planted it in regular Florida soil. Nothing special. Jujube is not picky. It grows in sand, loam, even clay.

We watered it regularly for the first few months, then backed off. Once it was established, we pretty much stopped watering it unless we were in a serious drought.

It grows upright and thorny. The branches have little spines, so we wear gloves when we prune it. But honestly, we do not prune it much. We just let it do its thing.

Jujube is deciduous, so it drops its leaves in winter and goes dormant. Do not panic when it looks dead. It is just resting. It will come back in spring.

And cold? Jujube handles it better than most tropical fruits. It can take freezes. It can handle temps down into the teens. In fact, it needs some chill hours to fruit well. So if you are in North Florida, jujube is perfect for you.

Varieties Worth Growing

Not all jujubes are the same. Some are better fresh. Some are better dried.

Li is the most popular variety. Big fruit, sweet, crisp. Great for eating fresh. This is the one most people plant.

Lang is another good one. Slightly smaller fruit but very sweet. Good fresh or dried.

Honey Jar is small but incredibly sweet. Like candy. The name is accurate.

Sugar Cane is long and cylindrical instead of round. Very sweet. Great for fresh eating.

We have got Li in our yard. Big, crisp, sweet. The kids eat them like apples.

What Can Go Wrong

Honestly? Not much.

Jujube has very few pests. Occasionally you might see aphids or fruit flies, but they are rare.

The thorns can be annoying. Wear gloves when you prune or harvest.

If you do not get enough chill hours in winter (below 45°F for a few weeks), the tree might not fruit as well. This is more of an issue in South Florida.

And birds like the fruit. But not as much as they like mulberries or cherries. You will still get plenty.

When to Harvest

Jujubes ripen in late summer to fall. The fruit starts green, then turns yellowish, then reddish-brown when fully ripe.

You can eat them at any stage. Green jujubes are crisp and tart like a green apple. Yellow jujubes are sweeter. Reddish-brown jujubes are the sweetest and have the best flavor.

Pick them when they are mostly brown with some red speckles. That is peak sweetness.

If you want to dry them, let them ripen fully on the tree until they start to wrinkle. Then pick them and dry them in the sun or a dehydrator.

Fresh jujubes last about a week in the fridge. Dried jujubes last for months.

How to Eat Them

Fresh jujubes? Eat them like an apple. Crisp, sweet, juicy. The skin is edible. The pit in the center is not.

Dried jujubes? Eat them like dates. Chewy, sweet, concentrated flavor. Great for snacking.

You can also cook with jujubes. Add them to soups, stews, teas. In Chinese medicine, jujubes are used in herbal teas for calming and digestion.

We eat ours fresh. The kids love them. They taste like candy but they are fruit. Win-win.

Why It Is Good for You

Jujubes are packed with vitamin C. More than oranges. Great for immunity.

High in antioxidants. Supports overall health and fights inflammation.

Good source of fiber. Helps with digestion.

Contains compounds that may help with anxiety and sleep. That is why jujube is used in traditional Chinese medicine.

And they are low in calories. You can eat a handful and not feel guilty.

Toni's Tip

We planted jujube because we wanted a fruit tree that did not need constant attention.

And that is exactly what we got. It grows. It fruits. It does not ask for much.

While I am out there babying the mangoes and the citrus and worrying about cold snaps, the jujube is just doing its thing. No drama. No fuss.

If you want a low-maintenance fruit tree that produces reliably, jujube is it.

Did You Know?

Jujube has been cultivated in China for over 4,000 years. It is also called Chinese date because dried jujubes look and taste similar to dates.

In Chinese medicine, jujube is used for calming the mind, improving sleep, and supporting digestion.

There are over 400 varieties of jujube worldwide. But in Florida, Li and Lang are the most popular.

And despite being called a date, jujube is not related to date palms at all. It is in the buckthorn family.

40. Soursop

The Tropical Giant I Killed Twice (But Finally Got Right)

Let me tell you about the plant that humbled me.

Soursop.

I have killed this tree twice. Twice. And I am not someone who kills plants easily.

The first time, I planted it in full sun thinking it would love the heat. It did not. The leaves burned. The tree struggled. It died.

The second time, I planted it in better soil but did not protect it from the cold. We got a frost. One night. That is all it took. Dead again.

But I was not giving up. Because I grew up drinking soursop juice. We called it *korosòl* in Creole. Thick, creamy, tropical, with this sweet-tart flavor that tastes like pineapple met strawberry and decided to make something completely unique.

This time around, I changed my strategy completely. I realized that in Central Florida, our "random" freezes are just too much for a young Soursop to handle in

the ground. So, I planted this one in a pot, and that has made all the difference.

40. Soursop

The power of the pot

Planting in a container was the best decision I made for this tree. It gives me total control. I filled it with rich, high quality soil and mulched it heavily to keep those roots happy. Because it is in a pot, I can move it to find that perfect sweet spot of partial shade. Soursop loves the heat, but that mid afternoon Florida sun can be a bit much for it when it is trying to establish itself. But the real "win" with the pot? Mobility.

What Makes Soursop Special

Soursop is huge. I am not talking about the tree (though it can get 15 to 20 feet tall). I am talking about the fruit.

One soursop can weigh 5 to 10 pounds. It is green, spiky on the outside, creamy white on the inside, with big black seeds you do not eat.

The flavor is tropical and complex. Sweet but tart. Creamy but refreshing. People describe it as pineapple-strawberry-banana-citrus all mixed together. But honestly, soursop tastes like soursop. There is nothing else like it.

We make soursop juice. Blend the pulp with water, strain out the seeds, add a little sugar if you want. Thick, creamy, incredible. In Haiti, we drink it cold on hot days. It is tradition.

You can also eat it fresh with a spoon. Or make soursop ice cream, smoothies, or even tea from the leaves.

But you have to grow it right. Because soursop does not forgive mistakes.

Why I Killed It Twice

Mistake number one: full sun.

I thought soursop would love full Florida sun. It did not. The leaves burned. The tree looked miserable. It died.

Soursop wants partial shade. Especially afternoon shade. It can handle some morning sun, but that brutal afternoon Florida sun? Too much.

Mistake number two: cold.

Soursop is tropical. Like really tropical. One frost and it is done. We got one cold night below 35°F and the tree died overnight.

Now I know: soursop cannot handle cold. Anything below 40°F and it starts to stress. Below freezing? You lose it.

So if you are in Central or North Florida and you get occasional freezes, you need to protect it. Cover it with blankets. Bring it inside if it is in a pot. Do something. Because cold will kill it fast.

What It Needs

Partial shade. Soursop does not want full blazing sun all day. Give it morning sun and afternoon shade.

Rich, moist soil. Lots of organic matter. Soursop is a heavy feeder.

Consistent watering. Do not let it dry out. Keep the soil evenly moist.

Mulch heavily to retain moisture and keep the roots cool.

Fertilizer every few months. Use a balanced fertilizer or compost. Soursop needs nutrients to produce those massive fruits.

Cold protection. This is critical. Soursop cannot handle freezes. Cover it or move it when temps drop below 45°F.

What Can Go Wrong

Cold will kill it. I cannot stress this enough. One frost and you are starting over.

Too much sun will burn the leaves. Plant it in partial shade.

If the soil dries out during fruiting, the fruit will drop. Keep it watered.

Aphids and scale can show up. Spray them off with water or use neem oil.

And here is the hard truth: soursop is picky. It does not forgive mistakes. You have to get the conditions right or it will struggle.

When to Harvest

Soursop fruits year-round in South Florida if conditions are right. In Central Florida, you will get fruit in summer and fall.

The fruit is ready when the spines soften and the skin turns slightly yellowish-green. If you press gently and it gives a little, it is ripe.

Do not wait too long. Overripe soursop gets mushy and ferments on the tree.

Pick it when it is just ripe, bring it inside, and let it finish ripening on the counter for a day or two if needed.

The fruit does not last long once ripe. Use it within a few days or freeze the pulp.

How to Use It

We make soursop juice. Scoop out the pulp, blend it with water, strain out the seeds and fibers, sweeten if you want. Thick, creamy, tropical. This is *korosòl.* This is tradition.

You can eat it fresh with a spoon. The texture is creamy and custard-like with a sweet-tart flavor.

You can make soursop ice cream, smoothies, or even soursop cheesecake.

And the leaves? People brew them into tea for relaxation and sleep. In Caribbean and Latin American cultures, soursop leaf tea is used for calming and digestion.

Why It Is Good for You

Soursop is high in vitamin C. Supports immunity and skin health.

Rich in antioxidants. Fights inflammation and supports overall health.

Good source of fiber. Helps with digestion.

Contains compounds that may help with relaxation and sleep. That is why soursop leaf tea is so popular.

And it is hydrating. Perfect for hot Florida days.

What No One Tells You

Soursop is not easy. It is picky about shade, soil, water, and temperature. You have to get it right.

Cold will kill it. One frost and you are done. Protect it or grow it in a pot you can move.

The fruit is massive. One soursop can weigh 5 to 10 pounds. You will have enough for juice, smoothies, and ice cream from one fruit.

It fruits year-round in South Florida. In Central Florida, you will get fruit in summer and fall if you protect it in winter.

And the flavor? There is nothing else like it. Sweet, tart, creamy, tropical. If you grew up drinking soursop juice, you know. If you did not, you are in for a treat.

Did You Know?

Soursop is native to the Caribbean and Central America. It has been cultivated for centuries.

In Haiti, we call it *korosòl*. In Spanish-speaking countries, it is *guanábana*. In English, soursop.

The leaves are used in traditional medicine for relaxation, sleep, and digestion. Soursop leaf tea is popular across the Caribbean and Latin America.

And despite being called soursop, the fruit is actually sweet with just a hint of tartness. The name comes from the slightly sour undertone in the flavor.

41. Everglades Tomato

The Wild Tomato That Survives Everything Florida Throws at It

I spent years fighting to grow tomatoes in Florida.

Every spring, I would plant cherry tomatoes, beefsteaks, heirlooms. I would baby them. Water them. Fertilize them. Watch them like a hawk.

And every summer, they would die. The heat would hit, the pests would show up, and my tomatoes would give up. Leaves would yellow. Fruit would stop. The plants would just quit.

I was so tired of losing tomatoes by June.

Then I found out about Everglades tomatoes. A wild tomato native to South Florida. A tomato that actually *wants* to grow here.

And I was like, wait. There is a tomato that thrives in Florida heat? That laughs at pests? That does not need me to baby it?

Yes. There is.

Everglades tomatoes are small, about the size of a marble. They taste sweet and tangy with a rich tomato flavor. And they grow like weeds. Seriously. Plant one and it will reseed itself and come back year after year.

No more starting over every spring. No more watching my tomatoes die in July. Everglades tomatoes just keep going.

Why Everglades Tomatoes Are Different

Most tomatoes are bred for cooler climates. They love spring. They tolerate early summer. But when Florida really heats up in July and August, they are done.

41. Everglades Tomato

Everglades tomatoes are native to South Florida. They evolved in our heat, our humidity, our pests. They are built for this.

They handle heat. The hotter it gets, the happier they are. While your beefsteaks are melting, Everglades tomatoes are still producing.

They resist pests. Aphids, whiteflies, hornworms—Everglades tomatoes shrug them off. They have natural resistance that most hybrid tomatoes do not have.

They reseed themselves. Drop a tomato on the ground and next spring you will have new plants popping up. You do not even have to replant.

And they are perennial in South Florida. They do not die after one season. They keep growing year after year.

This is the tomato Florida gardeners have been looking for.

How We Grow It

Our Everglades tomatoes live in full sun. They want all the light they can get.

We planted them in regular Florida soil. Nothing special. They are not picky.

We water them when they are young, then back off. Once established, they handle drought pretty well. We water during dry spells, but we do not baby them.

We do not fertilize much. Maybe some compost when we plant them, but that is it. Too much fertilizer makes them grow leaves instead of fruit.

And we let them sprawl. Everglades tomatoes grow like vines. They spread across the ground or climb if you give them something to grab onto. We put a tomato cage around ours just to keep them contained, but honestly, they do fine without it.

They reseed everywhere. We have Everglades tomatoes popping up in places we never planted them. The fruit drops, the seeds germinate, and boom—new tomato plants.

Cold? Everglades tomatoes can handle a light frost. They are tougher than most tomatoes. But a hard freeze will kill them. If you are in Central or North Florida and get freezes, they might not come back. But in South Florida, they are basically perennial.

What They Need

Full sun. At least 6 to 8 hours daily.

Well-draining soil. Everglades tomatoes do not like soggy roots, but they are not picky about soil type.

Moderate water. Water when young, then let them fend for themselves once established.

Minimal fertilizer. Too much nitrogen makes them grow leaves instead of fruit. Keep it light.

Space to sprawl. Everglades tomatoes spread. Give them room or cage them if you want to keep them contained.

What Can Go Wrong

Honestly, not much. This is one of the toughest plants you can grow.

Occasionally aphids or whiteflies show up, but Everglades tomatoes handle them better than hybrid tomatoes. The pests might show up, but they do not do much damage.

If you overwater or overfertilize, the plants will grow big and leafy but produce less fruit. Keep it lean.

Birds and squirrels like the fruit. But there is usually enough for everyone.

And if you are in North Florida with hard freezes, the plants might not survive winter. But in Central and South Florida, they keep going.

41. Everglades Tomato

When to Harvest

Everglades tomatoes fruit year-round in South Florida. Year. Round. No off-season. No waiting for spring.

In Central Florida, they fruit spring through fall, and sometimes even in winter if it stays warm.

The tomatoes are small—about the size of a marble or a cherry tomato. They turn red when ripe.

Pick them when they are fully red. They are sweet, tangy, and have a concentrated tomato flavor that hybrid tomatoes do not have.

You can eat them fresh, toss them in salads, roast them, or cook them down into sauce. They are small, but they pack flavor.

Why They Are Good for You

Everglades tomatoes are packed with vitamins A and C. Support immunity and skin health.

High in antioxidants, especially lycopene. Fights inflammation and supports heart health.

Good source of potassium and fiber.

And they are natural. No pesticides needed. No constant spraying. Just wild tomatoes doing their thing.

Did You Know?

Everglades tomatoes are native to South Florida. They are a wild species (*Solanum pimpinellifolium*) that evolved in the Everglades and coastal areas.

They are one of the most heat-tolerant and pest-resistant tomatoes in the world. Plant breeders use Everglades tomato genetics to create more resilient hybrid varieties.

In South Florida, you can find them growing wild in hammocks and along roadsides. They are naturalized and thrive without any human help.

And despite being wild, they taste incredible. Sweet, tangy, concentrated tomato flavor. This is what tomatoes are supposed to taste like.

41. Everglades Tomato

Now, I know some people find the Everglades tomato a little too tart or just too small to work with. If you are looking for that classic, big tomato taste but you still want a plant that won't quit on you the second the humidity hits ninety percent, you have some great options for our area. You just have to pick the varieties bred specifically for the heat.

The Heat Lovers

- **Heatmaster:** This one was literally bred for the Southeast. It is a determinate variety, meaning it grows to a certain size and then produces its fruit all at once. It is great for our area because it sets fruit even when the nights stay warm, which is usually where those big beefsteaks fail.
- **Solar Fire:** This is another superstar for Florida. It was developed by the University of Florida to resist the diseases that usually kill our plants in the summer. It produces a good sized, red tomato that stays firm even in the heat.
- **Tropic:** This is an heirloom variety that actually likes the humidity. Most heirlooms from up north will rot or get fungus the minute it rains, but Tropic was bred to handle the tropical climate. It gives you those large, sweet slicing tomatoes we all crave for sandwiches.
- **Neptune:** If you are gardening near the coast or in sandy soil, Neptune is a fantastic choice. It is highly resistant to bacterial wilt, which is a huge problem in Florida soil. It produces medium sized fruits that have a really well balanced, mild flavor.

A different kind of cherry

If you like the idea of a small tomato but want something a bit sweeter than the wild Everglades version, look for **Sun Sugar** or **Sweet 100**. These are hybrids, so they won't reseed and come back exactly the same like the Everglades ones do, but the flavor is like eating candy. They still handle the heat much better than a large slicer, so they are a safe bet for a long harvest.

Why variety matters

In Florida, the "window" for tomatoes is small. By picking these heat tolerant types, you are basically stretching that window by a few weeks or even months. While the Everglades tomato is the undisputed king of survival, these varieties give you that traditional garden tomato experience without the heartbreak of watching a plant die in June

42. Cuban Oregano

The Herb That Already Knows What You're Cooking

Cuban oregano is one of those herbs that smells like it already knows what you are cooking.

You brush past it in the garden and the whole yard smells like Sunday dinner. Like someone is already simmering beans with epis. Like the kitchen is calling you inside.

The leaves are thick and fuzzy. Almost succulent-like. You pinch one and the smell hits you immediately. Bold, aromatic, somewhere between oregano and thyme with a little bit of mint.

This is the herb that lives in every Haitian and Caribbean kitchen. The one your mom grabbed handfuls of without measuring. The one that made everything taste like home.

And the best part? It is ridiculously easy to grow in Florida.

Snap off a cutting. Stick it in the ground. It will root before you remember to water it. Seriously. Cuban oregano does not ask for much.

42. Cuban Oregano

Why It Works Here

Cuban oregano loves Florida's heat. The hotter it gets, the more aromatic the leaves become. While other herbs are struggling in July, Cuban oregano is thriving.

It does not care much about soil quality. Sand, loam, clay—it grows in all of it. Just give it sun and occasional water and it will take over.

It is drought-tolerant once established. You can forget to water it for a week and it will be fine.

It roots from cuttings easily. One plant becomes ten. You will have Cuban oregano everywhere. And you will give cuttings to everyone you know.

And it handles pests well. Bugs do not mess with it much. The strong aroma keeps most of them away.

How We Grow It

Our Cuban oregano lives in full sun to partial shade. It can handle both. We have some in full blazing sun and some under a tree with filtered light. Both are doing great.

We planted it in regular Florida soil. Nothing special. Cuban oregano is not picky.

We water it when we plant it, then mostly leave it alone. Once established, it handles drought pretty well. We water during serious dry spells, but that is it.

We pinch the tips often to keep it full and bushy. If you do not pinch it back, it gets leggy. But every time you pinch, you get more leaves. More branches. Bushier plant.

And we let it bloom sometimes. The flowers are pretty—little spikes of purple or white—and the bees love them. We pinch some blooms off to keep the plant producing leaves, but we leave a few for the pollinators.

Cuban oregano spreads. Not aggressively, but it spreads. If you do not want it taking over, grow it in a pot. We have it both in the ground and in pots. Both work.

What It Needs

Full sun to partial shade. Cuban oregano is flexible. It thrives in both.

Well-draining soil. It does not like soggy roots, but it is not picky about soil type.

Occasional water once established. Cuban oregano is drought-tolerant. Water it when you plant it, then back off.

Regular pinching to keep it bushy. Pinch the tips every few weeks. You will get more leaves and a fuller plant.

Cold? Cuban oregano can handle a light frost. But a hard freeze will damage it. If you are in Central or North Florida and get freezes, grow it in a pot you can bring inside. Or just take cuttings before winter and start fresh in spring.

When to Harvest

Harvest anytime the plant has enough leaves. You can start pinching within a few weeks of planting.

Just pinch or cut the tips. The plant will branch out and produce even more leaves.

Use the leaves fresh or dry them. Fresh Cuban oregano is more aromatic. Dried is still good but milder.

In the Kitchen

Cuban oregano belongs in Haitian and Caribbean cooking. It is bold. It is aromatic. It does not sit quietly in the background. It announces itself.

We use it in marinades for chicken, pork, and fish. A few leaves chopped up with garlic, lime, and oil. That is it.

We throw it in beans. Black beans, red beans, pigeon peas. Cuban oregano makes them taste like they simmered all day even if they did not.

We use it in rice and stews. Just a few leaves. Remember, it is strong.

And we make tea from the leaves. Cuban oregano tea is used in Caribbean cultures for colds, coughs, and digestion. Steep a few fresh leaves in hot water for 10 minutes. Add honey and lime if you want.

My mom used to grab handfuls of this without measuring. She just knew how much to use. That is the kind of herb Cuban oregano is. You cook with it enough and you just know.

42. Cuban Oregano

Why It Is Good for You

Cuban oregano has antibacterial and anti-inflammatory properties. It is used in traditional medicine across the Caribbean and Latin America.

The leaves contain compounds that may help with respiratory issues, colds, and coughs. That is why Cuban oregano tea is so popular during cold season.

It supports digestion. Drinking Cuban oregano tea after a heavy meal can help settle your stomach.

And it is natural. No pesticides needed. Just plant it and use it.

Did You Know?

Cuban oregano is not actually oregano. It is in the mint family. But the flavor is similar to oregano with hints of thyme and mint, which is why it is called Cuban oregano.

It is also called Mexican mint, Spanish thyme, or Indian borage depending on where you are.

It has been used in traditional medicine for centuries across the Caribbean, Latin America, and Asia.

And despite the name, it is not native to Cuba. It is native to southern and eastern Africa but has naturalized in tropical regions worldwide.

43. Chaya (Mexican Tree Spinach)

The Green That Does Not Ask Permission

I was so tired of fighting to keep greens alive in Florida.

Every spring, same story. I would plant kale, collards, Swiss chard. I would water them, mulch them, check on them every day. And they would do great. For a while.

Then summer would hit. The real Florida summer. And they would melt. Just give up. Leaves would turn yellow, bugs would move in, and by July I was pulling out dead plants and starting over.

Again.

I kept thinking, there has to be a green that actually wants to grow here.

Then someone mentioned chaya. Mexican tree spinach. A perennial that produces all year, handles heat, and does not care about pests.

I was like, sure. I have heard that before.

But I grabbed a cutting from a neighbor anyway. Stuck it in the ground. Watered it for a few weeks. Then mostly forgot about it.

And it took off.

Chaya grows tall. Like a small tree. Six, seven, eight feet if you let it. And it just keeps producing leaves. All year. No breaks. No drama.

But here is the catch: you cannot eat it raw. You have to cook the leaves first. Always. Raw chaya has compounds that will make you sick. But once you boil or sauté it? Perfectly safe. Tastes like spinach but richer.

Now we harvest from it every week. One plant gives us more greens than we can eat. And it does not ask for anything in return.

Why It Works in Florida

Chaya loves heat. The hotter it gets, the more it grows. While your lettuce is bolting and your kale is crispy, chaya is lush and green and producing.

It handles humidity. No mildew. No rot. Just steady growth.

It has very few pests. Occasionally you might see a caterpillar, but nothing serious. Chaya just grows without drama.

It is perennial. You plant it once and it keeps producing year after year. No replanting every season.

And it is productive. One plant gives you more greens than you can eat. We have one chaya plant and we harvest from it weekly.

How We Grow It

Our chaya lives in full sun to partial shade. It can handle both. We have it in a spot that gets morning sun and afternoon shade, and it is thriving.

We planted it from a cutting. That is how most people get chaya. You do not really find it at garden centers. You get a cutting from someone who already has it.

Stick a 6 to 8 inch woody cutting in moist soil. Water it regularly for the first few weeks. It will root. Then it will take off.

We do not fertilize much. Maybe some compost once or twice a year. Chaya does not need heavy feeding.

We water it regularly when it is young. Once established, it handles drought pretty well. We water during dry spells, but it does not need constant attention.

And we harvest often. The more you cut, the bushier it gets. If you do not harvest, it will get tall and leggy. But if you keep cutting the tips, it stays full and productive.

Chaya can get big. Like really big. Six to eight feet tall, just as wide. Give it space or be ready to prune it back.

Cold? Chaya does not love freezes. A light frost might knock it back, but it will regrow from the roots. A hard freeze can kill it. If you are in North or Central Florida and get regular freezes, grow it in a pot you can protect or just take cuttings before winter and start fresh in spring.

The One Rule You Cannot Break

Okay, listen. This is important.

You cannot eat chaya raw. You just cannot.

Raw chaya has compounds in it that will make you sick. Nausea, cramps, the whole deal. Not fun.

But when you cook it? Those compounds break down and disappear. The leaves become perfectly safe.

So here is what you do: boil the leaves for 5 to 10 minutes. Or sauté them. Or throw them in a soup or stew. Just cook them.

Do not eat them raw. Do not juice them raw. Do not throw them in a smoothie thinking you are being healthy. Cook them first.

I know it is an extra step. But it is not negotiable.

Once they are cooked, they taste like spinach. Mild, a little earthy, really good. But raw? No.

When to Harvest

Harvest anytime the plant has enough leaves. You can start harvesting within a few months of planting.

Just cut the tender tips. The top 6 to 8 inches of each branch. The plant will branch out and produce even more leaves.

Do not strip the whole plant. Just take what you need and let it keep growing.

We harvest weekly. Sometimes more if we are eating a lot of greens. The plant keeps up.

In the Kitchen

We boil chaya leaves for 5 to 10 minutes, then drain them. You can use that water to cook rice or beans if you want—it is full of nutrients.

Once cooked, chaya tastes mild and slightly earthy. Like spinach but richer.

We sauté it with garlic and olive oil. We add it to soups and stews. We mix it with rice and beans.

In Mexico and Central America, chaya is a staple green. People use it in tamales, soups, and as a cooked side dish.

My kids eat it mixed with rice and butter. They do not even question it. It is just greens.

43. Chaya (Mexican Tree Spinach)

Why It Is Good for You

Chaya is packed with vitamins and minerals. High in vitamins A, C, and several B vitamins. Good source of calcium, iron, and protein for a leafy green.

It supports digestion. High in fiber.

It is anti-inflammatory. Contains compounds that help reduce inflammation.

And it is nutrient-dense. More protein than most greens. More calcium than spinach.

In traditional medicine, chaya is used to support blood sugar regulation, digestion, and overall health.

But remember: always cook it first. Raw chaya is toxic. Cooked chaya is nutritious.

Did You Know?

Chaya has been cultivated in Mexico and Central America for centuries. It is a staple green in traditional Mayan cuisine.

The name "chaya" comes from the Mayan word for the plant.

It is sometimes called tree spinach because it grows tall like a small tree and the leaves taste similar to spinach when cooked.

And despite the toxins in raw leaves, cooked chaya is one of the most nutritious greens you can grow. More protein than spinach. More calcium than milk (per serving).

44. Calabaza

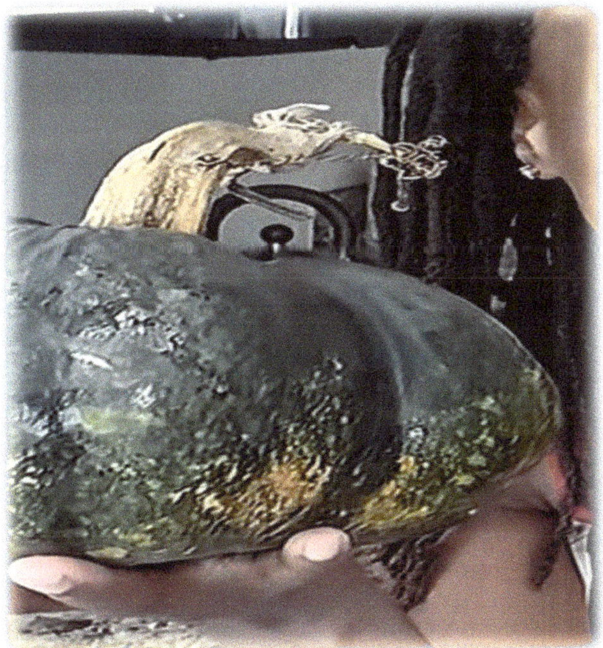

The Pumpkin That Tastes Like Home

Calabaza is a tropical pumpkin with bright orange flesh and a naturally sweet, nutty taste.

And if you grew up Haitian, you know exactly what calabaza means: soup joumou. The independence soup. The soup we make every January 1st to celebrate freedom.[23]

My mom made soup joumou every year. Big pot. Calabaza, beef, vegetables, pasta. It simmered all morning and the whole house smelled like comfort and history and pride.

---

[23] January 1st is **Haitian Independence Day**, and it is one of the most significant dates in world history. On January 1, 1804, Haiti officially declared its independence from France, becoming the first free black republic in the world and the first nation to permanently ban slavery. For us, this day is about more than just a historical date; it is a symbol of resilience, dignity, and the ultimate victory of the human spirit over oppression

44. Calabaza

Now I grow my own calabaza. And every time I cut one open and see that bright orange flesh, I think about my mom's kitchen. About tradition. About food that means something.

Calabaza loves Florida. It loves the heat, the sun, and plenty of space to run. And I mean run. The vines can cover a yard quickly. We planted one and it took over half the garden. Leaves everywhere. Flowers everywhere. And then, massive fruits.

Once they settle in, you will get pumpkins that store for months. We harvest in fall and use them all winter.

How We Grow It

Our calabaza lives in full sun. It wants every bit of light it can get.

We planted it in a spot with lots of space. Calabaza vines spread. They climb. They take over. Give them room or they will take it anyway.

We use a trellis for some of the vines to keep them from sprawling across the entire yard. But honestly, calabaza does what it wants.

We water regularly when the plants are young and flowering. Once the fruit sets, we back off a bit. Too much water can cause the fruit to split.

We do not fertilize heavily. Maybe some compost when we plant. Calabaza does not need much.

And we let the fruit ripen on the vine. You will know it is ready when the skin hardens and the vine starts to dry out. That is when you cut it.

Cold? Calabaza does not like freezes. It is a warm-season crop. Plant it in spring after the last frost. Harvest before the first frost in fall. In South Florida, you can grow it almost year-round.

What It Needs

Full sun. At least 6 to 8 hours daily.

Lots of space. Calabaza vines spread 10 to 15 feet or more. Do not plant it in a tiny corner.

Well-draining soil. Calabaza does not like wet feet.

Regular water when young and flowering. Back off once the fruit sets.

A trellis helps if you want to save space. But calabaza will sprawl if you let it.

44. Calabaza

When to Harvest

Calabaza takes 3 to 4 months from planting to harvest.

You will know it is ready when the skin hardens and turns a solid color (usually tan or light green on the outside). The vine will start to dry out near the fruit.

Cut the fruit with a few inches of stem attached. Do not yank it off.

Let it cure in the sun for a week or so to harden the skin even more. Then store it in a cool, dry place. Calabaza can last for months.

In the Kitchen

Calabaza is pure comfort food.

We roast cubes with garlic and herbs until they caramelize. Sweet, nutty, incredible.

We simmer it in coconut milk and thyme for a Haitian-style stew. The flavor deepens the longer you cook it.

And we make soup joumou. The Haitian independence soup. Calabaza, beef, vegetables, pasta, spices. It simmers for hours and every bite tastes like home.

The flesh is sweet and dense. You can use it anywhere you would use butternut squash or pumpkin. Soups, stews, roasted, mashed, baked into bread.

My kids eat it roasted with a little butter and cinnamon. They do not even know it is a vegetable.

Did You Know?

Calabaza is native to the Caribbean and Central America. It has been cultivated for thousands of years.

In Haiti, soup joumou is made every January 1st to celebrate independence. During slavery, Haitians were forbidden from eating this soup. After independence in 1804, soup joumou became a symbol of freedom.

Calabaza is also called West Indian pumpkin or Cuban squash.

And despite being called a pumpkin, calabaza tastes sweeter and nuttier than regular pumpkins. The flesh is denser and holds up better in soups and stews.

45. Cranberry Hibiscus

The Plant That Fools Everyone

Cranberry hibiscus is the plant that fools everyone into thinking it is only decorative.

People walk by our yard and stop to ask, "What is that gorgeous plant with the burgundy leaves?"

And I tell them, "Oh, that? That is salad."

They look at me like I am joking.

But I am not. Those burgundy leaves that glow in the sun? Edible. Tart and lemony. Like someone built a natural dressing right into the plant.

We grow cranberry hibiscus in the front yard. It is beautiful enough to be an ornamental. Deep burgundy leaves, pink flowers, tall and full. People think we hired a landscaper.

But we eat it.

Fresh leaves in salads. Boiled into tea with a little ginger and honey. The result? A ruby-colored drink that looks as good as it tastes.

Cranberry hibiscus is one of those plants that does double duty. It brings style and flavor in one go.

45. Cranberry Hibiscus

Why It Works Here

Cranberry hibiscus loves Florida heat. The hotter it gets, the deeper the burgundy color becomes.

It grows fast. You plant a cutting and within a few months it is tall and full.

It keeps giving as long as you trim it. The more you harvest, the bushier it gets.

It handles pests well. Bugs mostly leave it alone.

And it is beautiful. Front-yard worthy. People stop and stare.

How We Grow It

Our cranberry hibiscus lives in full sun to partial shade. We have some in full blazing sun and it is doing great. Deep burgundy, tall, full.

We planted it from cuttings. That is how most people get cranberry hibiscus. You do not really find it at garden centers. You get a cutting from someone who already has it.

Stick a 6 to 8 inch cutting in moist soil. Water it regularly for a few weeks. It will root. Then it will take off.

We water it regularly when it is young. Once established, it handles drought pretty well. We water during dry spells, but it does not need constant attention.

We trim it often to keep it full and bushy. The more you cut, the more it branches out. And every time you trim, you get more leaves to eat.

Cranberry hibiscus can get tall. Like 4 to 6 feet tall. If you do not want it that big, just keep trimming it back.

Cold? Cranberry hibiscus does not love freezes. A light frost might knock it back, but it will regrow from the roots. A hard freeze can kill it. If you are in Central or North Florida and get regular freezes, grow it in a pot you can protect or just take cuttings before winter and start fresh in spring.

When to Harvest

Harvest anytime the plant has enough leaves. You can start harvesting within a few months of planting.

Just pinch or cut the tender young leaves. They are the most flavorful and the least fibrous.

Older leaves are still edible but they get tougher. Better for tea than for salads.

We harvest weekly. The plant keeps up.

In the Kitchen

We use the young leaves fresh in salads. Chop them up and toss them in. They taste tart and lemony, like a natural vinaigrette built right in.

We make tea. Boil a handful of leaves in water for 10 to 15 minutes. Add ginger and honey if you want. The tea turns a beautiful ruby color. It tastes tart and refreshing. Perfect iced in summer.

You can also add the leaves to smoothies for a tart kick. Or sauté them with other greens.

My kids think the tea looks like magic. Ruby-colored and bright. They do not even care that it is good for them.

Why It Is Good for You

Cranberry hibiscus is high in antioxidants, especially anthocyanins. Those are the compounds that give the leaves their burgundy color.

It is anti-inflammatory. Supports overall health.

High in vitamin C and iron. Good for immunity and energy.

And it is hydrating. The tea is refreshing and packed with nutrients.

46. Avocado

Winning at Florida Gardening

Growing your own avocado feels like winning at Florida gardening.

I mean, you walk outside, pick a fresh avocado off your tree, bring it inside, and make toast. No store. No wondering if it is ripe. No squeezing twenty avocados trying to find one that is not rock hard or already brown inside.

Just fresh avocado. From your yard.

We planted our first avocado tree about five years ago. A Monroe. Someone told us Monroe does well in Florida because it handles humidity and produces big, creamy fruit.

And they were right.

But here is the thing: you have to be patient. It took three years before we got our first avocado. Three years of watering, mulching, protecting it from cold, and waiting.

But when that first fruit came in? We cut it open and it was perfect. Creamy, rich, buttery. A squeeze of lime and a pinch of salt. That is all you need.

Now we get avocados every year. And I will never look at a store avocado the same way again.

Florida-Friendly Varieties

Not all avocados do well in Florida. Some varieties need California's dry climate. Some need more chill hours than we get.

But there are varieties that love it here.

Monroe is one of the best. Big fruit, creamy texture, handles Florida humidity. This is what we have.

Lula is another solid choice. It produces well in Florida and the fruit is smooth and buttery.

Choquette is cold-hardy and productive. Good for Central and North Florida.

Brogdon is one of the most cold-tolerant avocados. It can handle temps down into the low 20s. If you are in North Florida, this is the one.

Most Florida avocados are larger and have a smoother, less nutty flavor than California avocados. But they are creamy and delicious.

How We Grow It

Our avocado lives in full sun. It wants all the light it can get.

We planted it in well-draining soil. Avocados hate wet feet. If the soil stays soggy, the roots will rot.

We mulch heavily around the base to protect the roots and retain moisture. But we keep the mulch a few inches away from the trunk. Avocado trunks need air.

We water regularly. Not constantly, but regularly. Avocados need steady moisture, especially when they are young and when they are fruiting. If the soil dries out too much, the fruit can drop.

And we protect it from cold. When it was young, we covered it with a blanket whenever temps dropped below 40°F. Now that it is mature, it can handle more cold. But we still keep an eye on the forecast.

Avocados can get big. Our Monroe is probably 15 feet tall and still growing. Give it space.

When to Harvest

Avocados do not ripen on the tree. They ripen after you pick them.

You will know they are ready to pick when the fruit is full-sized and the skin starts to change color slightly. For Monroe and Lula, the skin darkens a bit when ready.

Pick one and bring it inside. Let it sit on the counter for a few days. When it gives slightly when you press it, it is ripe.

If you pick too early, it will never ripen properly. If you wait too long, it will drop and split open on the ground.

We start testing in late summer. Pick one, wait a few days. If it ripens, the rest are ready. If it stays hard or tastes bad, wait another week and try again.

46. Avocado

Why It Is Good for You

Avocados are packed with healthy fats. Good for your heart, your brain, your skin.

High in potassium. More than bananas.

Good source of fiber. Supports digestion.

Rich in vitamins E, K, and B vitamins.

And they keep you full. Healthy fats and fiber mean you stay satisfied longer.

Did You Know?

Avocados are native to Central and South America. They have been cultivated for thousands of years.

Florida avocados are different from California avocados. Florida avocados are larger, smoother, and have a milder flavor. California avocados (like Hass) are smaller, bumpier, and nuttier.

Avocado trees can live and produce for decades. Some trees in Florida are over 50 years old and still fruiting.

And despite being called a vegetable, avocados are technically a fruit. A berry, to be specific.

47. Malabar Spinach

The Spinach That Actually Survives Florida Summer

Malabar spinach is the answer when Florida heat wipes out your regular spinach.

I spent years trying to grow spinach in Florida. Every spring, same story. I would plant spinach, baby it, water it, check on it every day. And it would do great. For about six weeks.

Then the heat would hit. Real Florida heat. And the spinach would bolt. Just shoot up a flower stalk and quit making leaves. Done. Over. By May, I was pulling out dead spinach plants.

Every. Single. Year.

Then someone told me about Malabar spinach. Not actually spinach, but it tastes similar and it thrives in heat.

I was skeptical. A spinach that loves summer? In Florida? Sure.

But I planted it anyway. Gave it a fence to climb. Watered it. And walked away.

And it took off.

Malabar spinach climbs instead of growing low. The shiny leaves stay crisp and tender even in midsummer. It does not bolt. It does not quit. It just keeps producing.

Now we harvest from it all summer long. While everyone else's spinach is dead, ours is climbing the fence and looking gorgeous.

Why It Works Here

Malabar spinach loves heat. The hotter it gets, the better it grows. This is the opposite of regular spinach.

It climbs. Give it a fence or trellis and it will reward you until the weather cools down.

The leaves stay tender even in July and August. No bitterness. No toughness.

It is beautiful. Glossy green leaves, pink stems. One of the prettiest edible plants you can grow.

And it produces all summer. No bolting. No quitting. Just steady production.

47. Malabar Spinach

How We Grow It

Our Malabar spinach lives in full sun to partial shade. We have it on a fence in partial shade and it is doing great.

We planted it from seeds. You can also find starter plants sometimes. It grows fast either way.

We gave it a fence to climb. Malabar spinach is a vine. It needs something to grab onto. A fence, a trellis, anything vertical.

We water it regularly. Malabar spinach does not like to dry out completely. Keep the soil consistently moist, especially during hot months.

We harvest often. The more you pick, the more it produces. Just pinch off the tender tips and leaves. The plant keeps growing.

And we let it reseed. At the end of summer, Malabar spinach produces small purple berries. If you let them drop, new plants will come up next spring. Or you can collect the seeds and plant them yourself.

Cold? Malabar spinach is a warm-season plant. It dies back in winter. But if you let it reseed or save seeds, you can replant in spring.

What It Needs

Full sun to partial shade. Malabar spinach can handle both. Partial shade is nice in the hottest part of summer.

Consistent moisture. Do not let it dry out completely. Keep the soil moist, especially during hot weather.

Regular harvesting. The more you pick, the more it produces.

If the soil dries out too much, the leaves can get tough. Keep it watered.

If you do not give it something to climb, it will sprawl on the ground. It still grows, but it is easier to manage on a trellis.

Cold will kill it. Malabar spinach is a warm-season plant. It dies back in winter. But it reseeds easily, so you can have it again next year.

And here is the thing: Malabar spinach has a slightly mucilaginous texture when cooked. Like okra. Some people love it. Some people do not. If you do not like that texture, use it raw or add it at the very end of cooking.

When to Harvest

Harvest anytime the plant has enough leaves. You can start harvesting within a few weeks of planting.

Just pinch off the tender young leaves and tips. The plant will branch out and produce even more.

We harvest weekly all summer long. The plant keeps up.

Older leaves are still edible but they get thicker. Better cooked than raw.

In the Kitchen

We use the young leaves fresh in salads. They taste mild and slightly citrusy. Perfect for adding crunch and color.

We add them at the end of cooking to keep that bright green color. Toss them into stir-fries, soups, or sautéed dishes right before serving.

If you cook them too long, they get a little slimy like okra. Some people love that. Some people do not. If you do not, just use them raw or barely cook them.

My kids eat the pink stems. They think they look cool. And honestly, they do. Pink stems and glossy green leaves make every salad look fancy.

Why It Is Good for You

Malabar spinach is high in vitamins A and C. Supports immunity and skin health.

Good source of calcium and iron. Supports bone health and energy.

High in fiber. Helps with digestion.

And it is low in calories. You can eat a whole bowl and not feel guilty.

Did You Know?

Malabar spinach is native to tropical Asia. It has been cultivated for centuries in India and Southeast Asia.

It is also called Ceylon spinach, climbing spinach, or vine spinach.

The purple berries can be used as a natural dye. They stain everything purple. So if you are handling them, be prepared.

47. Malabar Spinach

And despite being called spinach, it is not related to regular spinach at all. It is in the Basellaceae family. But the leaves taste similar enough that the name stuck.

48. Sweet Potato

The Underground Treasure Hunt

Sweet potatoes are the ultimate overachiever for a Florida backyard. If you have a patch of sandy dirt where nothing else wants to grow, throw some sweet potato slips there and get out of the way. They love the heat, they don't mind our soil, and they double as a beautiful groundcover that chokes out weeds. But I will be the first to tell you: the harvest is where the drama happens. It is a total guessing game, and sometimes you dig up a "treasure" that looks like it went through a paper shredder.

Getting them in the ground

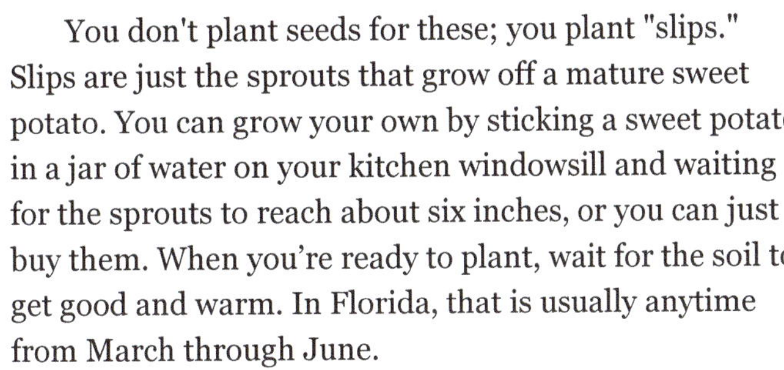

You don't plant seeds for these; you plant "slips." Slips are just the sprouts that grow off a mature sweet potato. You can grow your own by sticking a sweet potato in a jar of water on your kitchen windowsill and waiting for the sprouts to reach about six inches, or you can just buy them. When you're ready to plant, wait for the soil to get good and warm. In Florida, that is usually anytime from March through June.

Sweet potatoes are not picky, but they do want loose, sandy soil. If your dirt is packed as hard as a brick, those potatoes are going to be stunted and misshapen. I like to build up long mounds or "hills" about twelve inches high. Dig a small hole every eighteen inches along the mound and tuck your slip in deep, leaving just the top few leaves poking out. Giving them that raised, loose soil makes it so much easier for the tubers to expand—and way easier for you to dig them up later.

Keeping the vines happy

Once they are in, give them a good soak. You want to keep the soil consistently moist for the first week or two while they establish their roots. After that? You can pretty much back off. Sweet potatoes are tough; they can handle a dry spell better than almost anything else in the garden. Just give them a deep drink during those weeks when the Florida sun is really beating down and we aren't getting our afternoon rain.

Don't go crazy with the fertilizer, either. If you give them too much nitrogen, you are going to have the most beautiful, lush green vines in the neighborhood, but when you go to dig, you'll find tiny, pathetic roots. They need that "struggle" to put their energy into the tubers. I usually just mix in a little compost at the start and let them fend for themselves. These plants are the definition of "set it and forget it."

The Guessing Game: When to Pull?

Unlike a tomato that turns red or a pepper that gets shiny, sweet potatoes don't give you a clear signal. They are hiding underground, minding their business. If you pull them too early, you get "fingerlings" that aren't worth the effort to peel. If you wait too long, they can get massive, woody, and prone to cracking.

I usually mark my calendar for about four months—or 100 to 120 days—after planting. Since I don't have time to be a perfectionist, I look for the vines to start yellowing just a little bit, then I do a "test dig." I'll gently move the soil away from the base of a plant with my hands. If I see a potato that looks like a decent meal, it is time. Just remember, once our Central Florida rains get too heavy or we hit a cold snap, those tubers will start to rot, so don't push your luck.

To Store-Bought or Not? The Sweet Potato Dilemma

When you're ready to grow your own slips, you have a choice: buy them from a reputable nursery or try to sprout a sweet potato you bought at the grocery store. I've done both, and here is the honest truth about why it matters.

The Problem with Non-Organic

If you grab a regular, non-organic sweet potato from the produce bin at a big chain store, you might be waiting forever for it to sprout. Most of those are treated with a "sprout inhibitor"—a chemical spray meant to keep the potato looking pretty and shelf-stable in the store. It's great for the grocer, but it's a nightmare for the gardener. That potato is essentially "asleep" and it's fighting against the chemical to wake up. Sometimes they never sprout at all; they just sit in the jar and rot.

Why Organic is the Way to Go

If you're going the grocery store route, always buy **organic**. Organic farmers don't use those sprout inhibitors. When you put an organic sweet potato in water or moist soil, it knows exactly what to do. It'll push out those purple and green sprouts much faster and more reliably because it hasn't been chemically "turned off." Plus, since you're planning on eating the leaves and the tubers later, you're starting with a clean slate without those systemic chemicals in the plant's DNA.

The Nursery Advantage

Now, the "fancy" way is to buy certified slips from a nursery. The big benefit here isn't just about chemicals; it's about **disease**. Sweet potatoes can carry viruses and pests like the weevil I mentioned earlier. Certified slips are screened to make sure they are clean. Also, when you buy from a nursery, you get to pick a specific variety—like a deep purple one or a super sweet Beauregard—instead of just whatever "orange potato" the store happened to have in stock.

The Mystery of the Holes

There is nothing more heartbreaking than digging up a beautiful, plump sweet potato only to find it covered in tiny, deep holes. It looks like someone went at it with a tiny drill bit. That is usually the work of the sweet potato weevil. These pests are sneaky because you won't see them on the leaves; they do all their damage under the surface.

If you find holes in your harvest, it usually means the potatoes stayed in the ground a little too long, giving the larvae more time to feast. My fix for this is to keep the soil hilled up high around the base of the plants. Keeping those tubers buried deep makes it much harder for the weevils to reach them. If you've struggled with this, try harvesting a week or two earlier next time.

Why They Work for a Busy Life

I don't have time to babysit plants. Sweet potatoes are exactly that. You don't plant seeds; you plant "slips," which are just sprouts from a potato. You can grow your own in a jar of water on the counter, which the kids love to watch. Once the sprouts are about six inches long, you just snap them off and stick them in the dirt.

The "Wait" After the Harvest

Here is the part that tests my patience: do not eat them the day you dig them up. If you bake a sweet potato right out of the ground, it will be starchy and kind of bland. They need to "cure." I lay mine out in a warm, dry, shaded spot for about two weeks. This lets the starches turn into sugars and helps the skin toughen up so they last longer. It is a long wait, but that two week rest is the difference between a "meh" potato and a "wow" potato.

The Secret Second Harvest: Eating the Leaves

Most people grow sweet potatoes for what's happening underground, but they are missing out on the best part. The leaves are actually 100% edible, and in my kitchen, they are a lifesaver. While you are waiting four months for those tubers to grow, you can harvest the greens all summer long.

Unlike regular potato leaves, which are toxic, sweet potato leaves are packed with nutrients. They are a powerhouse of vitamins A, C, and K, and they have more antioxidants than many of our favorite "superfood" greens. They have a mild, slightly sweet flavor that doesn't have that "iron" aftertaste you sometimes get with spinach.

How to use them

I treat them just like spinach or kale. You can toss the young, tender leaves directly into a salad, but they are best when they are lightly sautéed. I'll chop them up and wilt them into a stir-fry with a little garlic and onion, or throw a handful into a smoothie for the kids. Because they grow so fast in the Florida heat, you can clip them back regularly and the plant will just keep pushing out more. It is basically an endless supply of summer greens that won't bolt when the sun gets disrespectful.

Toni's Tip

Because the vines spread like crazy, I use sweet potatoes as a "living mulch" under my larger fruit trees. They keep the ground cool and the weeds down, and at the end of the season, I get a bonus harvest of tubers. It is the ultimate two for one deal for a gardener who likes things simple and productive.

49. Seminole Pumpkin

The Two Seeds That Changed Everything

I was sleeping on this pumpkin for years.

We had just run out of sweet potatoes. And I was spending hundreds of dollars every month on baby food. Those little jars and pouches. You know the ones. Mostly water. A tiny bit of actual food. And expensive.

I kept looking at those jars thinking, "Why am I doing this? I have a whole garden."

So I planted two Seminole pumpkin seeds. Two. That is it.

And man, the amount we got back with little help from me.

The vines took off. They climbed the fence, wrapped around trees, spread across half the yard. I barely touched them. I watered when I remembered. I did not fertilize. I just let them grow.

And they produced. One plant gave us maybe 15 pumpkins. The other gave us more. Big, smooth, tan pumpkins that stored for months.

49. Seminole Pumpkin

I cooked them down, mashed them, and froze them in portions. Baby food. Toddler food. Food for all of us. Rich, sweet, orange flesh that tasted like butternut squash but better.

No more spending hundreds on jars of water. Just pumpkins from two seeds.

If Florida had a plant that tells the story of strength and survival, it would be the Seminole pumpkin. This pumpkin has been growing here for centuries. Long before grocery stores. Long before baby food aisles.

The Seminole people grew this pumpkin. It fed them. It sustained them. And it is still here, thriving in Florida's sandy soil and brutal heat, because it was built for this place.

Seminole pumpkin is not a plant you control. It is a plant you let roam. The vines stretch far, climbing fences, wrapping around trees, spreading across the ground. If you try to contain it, you will lose. Just give it space and let it do what it has been doing for hundreds of years.

The fruit is smooth, tan, and shaped like a drop of sunshine. Inside, the flesh is deep orange and sweet, with a rich, buttery flavor. Like butternut squash but even more complex. Deeper. Richer.

49. Seminole Pumpkin

Once harvested, the pumpkins can last for months without losing flavor. We pick them in fall and use them all winter.

This is more than a crop. This is a Florida heirloom. It reminds us that good things take time, patience, and respect for the land.

Why It Belongs Here

Seminole pumpkin loves sandy soil. The kind of soil most vegetables hate. But Seminole pumpkin? It thrives.

It loves heat. While other squash are wilting in July, Seminole pumpkin is growing strong.

It handles pests well. Squash bugs and vine borers that destroy other pumpkins? Seminole pumpkin shrugs them off.

It needs freedom to roam. The vines can stretch 20 to 30 feet or more. They climb, they spread, they go wherever they want.

And it produces. One plant can give you 10 to 20 pumpkins. Sometimes more.

49. Seminole Pumpkin

How We Grow It

Our Seminole pumpkin lives in full sun. It wants every bit of light it can get.

We planted it in spring when the soil warmed up. Seminole pumpkin needs warm soil to germinate. Do not rush it. Wait until after the last frost and the ground is warm.

We planted the seeds in mounds. A few seeds per mound, about 6 feet apart. The vines will fill in the space. Trust me.

We watered regularly when the plants were young. Once established, Seminole pumpkin is drought-tolerant. It does not need constant watering.

And we let it roam. The vines climb our fence, wrap around trees, spread across the ground. We do not try to control it. We just let it grow.

Seminole pumpkin does not need much. Some sun, some space, some time. That is it.

When to Harvest

Seminole pumpkin takes 3 to 4 months from planting to harvest.

You will know it is ready when the skin hardens and the vine starts to dry out near the fruit. The pumpkin will turn from green to tan.

Cut the fruit with a few inches of stem attached. Do not yank it off.

Let it cure in the sun for a week or two. This hardens the skin even more and helps it store longer.

Then store it in a cool, dry place. Seminole pumpkins can last for months. We have had them last 6 months or more without going bad.

In the Kitchen

The flesh is deep orange and sweet. Rich and buttery. Like butternut squash but better.

We roast slices with olive oil and salt until they caramelize. Sweet, rich, incredible.

We mash it into soup with coconut milk and ginger. The flavor deepens when cooked and the aroma fills the kitchen with warmth.

We blend it into pie filling. Seminole pumpkin makes the best pumpkin pie. Hands down.

My kids eat it roasted with butter and cinnamon. They do not even know it is healthy.

Why It Is Good for You

Seminole pumpkin is high in vitamins A and C. Supports immunity and skin health.

Rich in fiber. Helps with digestion.

Good source of potassium and magnesium. Supports heart health and energy.

And it is low in calories. You can eat a whole bowl and not feel guilty.

Did You Know?

Seminole pumpkin has been cultivated by the Seminole people for centuries. It is a Florida native crop that predates European settlement.

The pumpkin is incredibly well-adapted to Florida's climate. It handles heat, pests, and sandy soil better than almost any other squash.

It is also called Seminole squash or Florida Seminole pumpkin.

And despite being called a pumpkin, it is technically a squash. But the name stuck because of its rich, sweet flavor and how it is used in cooking.

50. Taro

Taro thrives in places most plants avoid. Got a low spot in your yard that stays soggy? Plant taro there. Got a pond edge that is always wet or a patch of partial shade where nothing else wants to grow? Plant taro there. Taro loves what other plants hate: heavy soil, warm humid air, and shade.

We have a low spot in our yard that floods every time it rains. I spent years trying to grow things there, but everything would rot. The roots would sit in water and die. Then someone told me to try taro. I was skeptical, but I planted it anyway, and it took off. Now that "problem" spot is one of the most productive parts of our yard.

Why it works for Florida

The roots are starchy like potatoes but with a light, nutty flavor. They soak up flavor beautifully, and when cooked right, they feel silky and rich. Taro loves our heat and humidity; the warmer and more humid it gets, the better it grows. It is also incredibly flexible when it comes to light. Most vegetables demand full sun, but taro does just fine with some shade. Plus, those big heart-shaped leaves make your garden look like a tropical paradise. It is the ultimate low-maintenance solution: plant it in the mud and let it do its thing.

How we grow it

We planted taro corms—those are the root pieces—about four to six inches deep in our low spot. You can find these at Asian markets or online. We just stuck them in, watered them once, and walked away. Taro does not need much, and we don't even fertilize heavily—maybe some compost once or twice a year. In Central Florida, it might die back during a hard freeze in winter, but it usually regrows from the roots in spring. In South Florida, you can keep it going year round.

50. Taro

The Elephant Ear Trap

Walk around any neighborhood in Florida and you'll see massive, heart-shaped leaves that look exactly like taro. People call them "Elephant Ears," and while they look the same, do not go digging up your neighbor's landscaping for dinner. There are plenty of ornamental varieties out there that are purely for show and can be even more irritating to your throat than the real deal. My rule is simple: only plant what you've sourced from a reputable food seller or the produce aisle of an Asian market. If you didn't buy it to eat it, don't put it in your food forest.

The harvest and the kitchen

Taro takes about six to nine months to mature. You'll know it's ready when the leaves start to yellow and die back. Dig up the corms carefully—they are usually about six to twelve inches underground—wash them, and store them in a cool, dry place. My kids eat it mashed with butter and herbs; they think it's mashed potatoes, and I don't correct them. It's high in fiber, potassium, and vitamins C and E, so it's a powerhouse for the family. Just remember to save some of the smaller corms to replant so you have a crop ready for next year.

The Bonus Harvest: Taro Leaves

Since we're big on not wasting anything in this garden, let's talk about the leaves. They are 100% edible and a staple in Caribbean cooking, but the "always cook it" rule goes double here. You can't just give these a quick sauté like spinach. They need a long, slow simmer—usually at least 45 minutes—to break down those scratchy crystals. Once they're done, they have this deep, earthy flavor and a silky texture that is incredible in soups. It's a great way to get a harvest while you're waiting months for the roots to be ready.

The one rule you cannot break

I have to be very direct about this: always cook taro before eating it. Raw taro contains calcium oxalate crystals that will irritate your mouth and throat. It is not a fun experience. Cooking breaks down those crystals and makes it perfectly safe. Whether you boil it, steam it, roast it, or fry it, just make sure heat is involved before it hits the plate. Do not juice it raw and do not toss raw pieces into a salad.

No Pond? No Problem.

You don't need a flooded backyard to grow this. If your yard is as dry as a bone, you can grow taro in a five-gallon bucket. The trick is to use a bucket with no drainage holes. Fill it with rich soil, plant your root, and keep the water topped off so the soil stays like thick mud. It's the perfect way to get that tropical look on a patio or in a small space without having to dig a hole or wait for a rainstorm to flood your yard.

Toni's Tip

Because my gardening style is a little chaotic, I love plants that solve problems for me. Taro turned a "dead zone" in my yard into a lush, tropical food source. If you have a spot where nothing else survives, stop fighting nature and plant taro. It's beautiful enough to be an ornamental plant, but it works hard enough to feed your family.

51. Yardlong Beans

Yardlong beans are the vines that never stop showing off. The pods can grow up to three feet long. Three feet! They hang from the trellis like garden ribbons.

People walk by our yard and stop mid step. They always ask, "What are those?" and when I say "Beans," they do not believe me. Most people think beans only get a few inches long, but yardlong beans are different. We planted them one spring because we were tired of regular green beans giving up in the heat. By June, our standard bush beans were done, finished, and dead. But yardlong beans? They love the heat. The hotter it gets, the more they produce.

Why they work for Florida

While regular green beans quit in the summer, yardlong beans thrive. They are fast climbers that will take over a trellis in weeks. One of the best things about them is that they stay crisp even after cooking. They do not get mushy or soggy like some varieties. They are the definition of abundance: the more you pick, the more the plant pushes out. It is that simple. You keep harvesting, and they keep rewarding you with more "garden art" hanging from your vines.

How we grow them

Our yardlong beans live in full sun because they want all the light they can get. We plant them from seeds directly in the ground or in large pots once the soil is good and warm in the spring. You have to give them a strong trellis. Do not go cheap on the support because these vines get heavy once those pods start coming. We water them regularly when they are young and flowering, and once they start producing, we keep the soil consistently moist. If you are in Central or South Florida, these will carry you all the way through the summer and into the fall.

The kitchen and the harvest

Here is the secret: even though they *can* grow to three feet, you want to harvest them when they are about 12 to 18 inches long. That is when they are the most tender and sweet. The beans should be firm and snap easily when you bend them. If they feel limp or tough, you waited too long. We harvest every two or three days during the peak season.

In the kitchen, I've had to get creative. I remember seeing a recipe on the Food Network once and thinking I could make it work with what was growing on my trellis. Now, I sauté them with a little sesame oil, garlic, and ginger. They stay firm and flavorful instead of turning into mush. My kids even eat them like French fries when they are roasted with a little salt.

Why they are good for you

These beans are a powerhouse for the family. They are high in fiber, a great source of vitamins A and C, and they even pack some protein and iron. They are naturally low in calories and because they are so pest resistant in our climate, you do not have to worry about spraying them with anything crazy. It is just clean, healthy food that grows like a weed in the Florida sun.

Toni's Tip

If you are tired of your garden quitting on you in June, you need yardlong beans. They do not hold back and they do not ask for much other than a sturdy place to climb. Because they are actually related to black eyed peas rather than standard green beans, they have that tropical resilience built into their DNA. Plant them, pick them often, and enjoy the show. Your neighbors will definitely have something to talk about when they see three foot beans hanging over your fence.

52. Jackfruit

The Tree That Grows Meat (Sort Of)

The first time I saw a jackfruit tree producing, I could not believe what I was looking at. I was at a friend's house and there it was: fruit growing directly on the trunk. Not on the branches, but on the trunk. And it was massive. We are talking thirty, forty, fifty pounds massive. It was just hanging there like the tree had decided to wear a suit of armor. I walked around it trying to figure out how it was even possible for a tree to hold that much weight without snapping. My friend just laughed and said, "That is what jackfruit does."

I was sold right then and there. I need this tree. Here is why: one jackfruit can feed a whole family. When it is ripe, the flesh is sweet and tropical. When it is green, it is starchy and meaty. People call green jackfruit a meat substitute because of the texture, and they are not lying. Ripe jackfruit tastes like a mix between pineapple, mango, and banana with a bubblegum aroma that fills the whole kitchen. Because a tree that grows meat and feeds a family from one fruit is exactly the kind of tree I need in my yard.

Why it works for Florida

Jackfruit loves our heat and humidity. The hotter it gets, the better it grows. Because it produces such massive fruit—sometimes weighing up to eighty pounds—it has to grow on the trunk and the thickest main branches. This is a wild look called cauliflory, and it is how the tree supports that kind of weight. It is incredibly versatile because you can use it as a savory main dish when it is green or a sweet dessert when it is ripe. You will have jackfruit for days.

How to grow your own

From what I have learned through months of research, jackfruit trees want full sun and all the light they can get. They need rich soil with plenty of compost, but they do not want to sit in water. If you have heavy clay, plant it on a mound to keep those roots happy. Water regularly when it is young and during the fruiting season, and mulch heavily to keep things cool.

Here is the critical part for us in Central Florida: protect it from the cold. When it is a baby tree, cover it with blankets whenever the temperature drops below 40°F. Once it is mature, it can handle more of a chill, but those early years are vital. Jackfruit trees can get thirty to forty feet tall, so give it space or be ready to prune it to keep it manageable. It takes about three to five years to see your first fruit, but it is worth the wait.

The harvest and the "sticky" reality

You will know a jackfruit is ripe when the skin shifts from green to a yellowish green and the spines soften slightly. You will also smell it before you see it. For green jackfruit to use as a meat substitute, harvest it while it is firm and still green. You have to cut the fruit from the tree with a sharp knife; do not try to twist it off or you will damage the tree.

Now, for the part no one tells you: jackfruit is sticky. There is a latex inside that will coat your hands, your knife, and your cutting board. Oil everything before you start cutting to keep the mess under control. One fruit is a lot to handle, so be ready to eat jackfruit for breakfast, lunch, and dinner. Also, do not throw away the seeds! You can boil them like chestnuts, and they taste nutty and starchy.

Why it belongs in your yard

It is high in vitamin C, packed with fiber, and full of antioxidants. It is naturally filling and nutritious. My research keeps telling me one thing: one tree is enough. You do not need five; you need one. Maybe two if you have a massive family to feed. This is a survival food in many parts of the world because one tree can produce hundreds of pounds of food every year.

Toni's Tip

I have picked my spot: full sun, lots of space, and protected from the wind. Now I just need to get it in the ground. If you are wondering about pots, here is the hard truth: you really cannot grow a jackfruit to full production in a container. They just get too big and the fruit is too heavy. This is a tree that needs its space to truly show off. It takes patience, but when you are serving up a "pulled pork" sandwich made from fruit you grew yourself, you will understand why people wait years for that first harvest.

52. Jackfruit

Did You Know?

Jackfruit is the largest tree-borne fruit in the world. One fruit can weigh up to 100 pounds.

It is native to South and Southeast Asia and has been cultivated for thousands of years.

In many tropical countries, jackfruit is considered a survival food because one tree can produce hundreds of pounds of fruit per year.

And despite being called a meat substitute when green, ripe jackfruit is one of the sweetest tropical fruits you can grow.

53. Sapodilla

The Tree I Took for Granted

I had a sapodilla tree in my backyard when we lived in Hollywood, and I had no idea what I had. It was just there, this sturdy tree with brown, rough skinned fruit. I would pick them sometimes, but I did not think much of it. Then the Jamaican neighbors started showing up, asking if they could pick some and filling bags. They were going crazy over this fruit. I was like, "Really? This tree?" And they would tell me, "You do not know what you have. This is sapodilla. This is gold."

The Taste of Backyard Gold

When you bite into a sapodilla, you aren't just eating fruit. You are eating brown sugar and caramel that grew on a tree. There is no other way to describe it. The flesh is a deep, warm tan color, and the texture is slightly grainy, very similar to a perfectly ripe pear. It is incredibly sweet, but not in a sharp way like a citrus fruit. It is a rich, malty sweetness that lingers.

Every time I scoop some out with a spoon, I am reminded that nature really did make its own version of candy.

If you have a sweet tooth like I do, this is a great tree to have in your yard. Most fruit trees give you something tart or refreshing, but sapodilla is different. It is like having a direct line to a bakery. There is no tang, no acidity, and zero pucker factor. It is just smooth, unapologetic sweetness. When that afternoon craving hits and I want something sugary, I can just grab one of these. It satisfies that "I need a dessert" feeling without me having to reach for a candy bar or bake a tray of cookies. It is nature's way of looking out for those of us who would live on brown sugar if we could.

Why I Miss That Tree

Now that I don't have that tree in my yard, I realize how much I relied on it. I miss the convenience of walking into my own backyard and having a gift ready to give to my neighbors. I miss the way the tree looked, lush, green, and sturdy, even when the Florida weather got rough. But mostly, I miss the connection. In Hollywood, that tree was a bridge between me and the neighbors I might never have talked to otherwise. It made my yard a destination.

Now, when I see sapodilla at the market for five or six dollars a pound, I think about how I used to let it drop on the ground because I didn't know what I had. The Jamaicans were right. I had gold in my backyard and I did not even know it. So now I am going to plant another one. You do not know what you have until it is gone.

Why It Works for Florida

Sapodilla loves Florida's heat and humidity. It thrives here and it is incredibly low maintenance. Once it is established, it does not need much from you. It handles pests well, so you won't see many bugs bothering it, and it is self fertile, meaning you only need one tree to get fruit. It produces reliably year after year, so once it starts, you are set.

How to Grow Your Own

From what I have learned, sapodilla loves full sun and wants all the light it can get. You plant it in well draining soil, it does not like to sit in water, but it is not picky about the type of soil. Whether you have sand, loam, or even a bit of clay, it grows in all of it. You water it regularly when it is young, but once it is established, it is surprisingly drought tolerant.

Mulch around the base to keep the roots cool and just let it grow. It does not need heavy pruning, though you can trim it to keep it manageable. Left alone, it can get thirty to fifty feet tall, but you can keep it pruned to fifteen or twenty feet and it will still produce plenty of fruit for your family.

The Waiting Game and the Harvest

The hardest part about sapodilla is the patience required. You might be waiting five to eight years for your first harvest, but it is worth every second. One thing you have to remember: sapodilla fruit does not ripen on the tree. You have to pick it and let it soften inside.

You will know it is ready to pick when the fruit is full sized and the skin starts to look slightly dull instead of shiny. Bring it inside and let it sit on the counter for a few days. When it gives slightly when you press it, it is ripe. If you pick it too early, it will never ripen properly. If you wait too long, it will drop and split on the ground. We start testing in late summer, pick one, wait a few days, and if it ripens, the rest are ready.

In the Kitchen

We eat sapodilla fresh. You just cut it in half and scoop out the flesh with a spoon. The seeds are big, black, and have a little hook on them, so do not eat those, just scoop around them. Because the flavor is so naturally sweet, you can blend it into smoothies or even make ice cream without needing much extra sugar. My kids eat it fresh and think it tastes like candy, which it basically is.

Toni's Tip

I had gold in my backyard and I took it for granted. The neighbors knew, but I had to lose it to appreciate it. If you are looking for one of the easiest, most reliable tropical fruit trees for Florida, this is it. It is native to Central America and the Caribbean, and it even produces chicle, the natural gum used to make chewing gum before the synthetic stuff took over. Plant one, be patient with it, and I promise you will appreciate it every time you walk into your backyard.

54. Longan

Lychee's Easier Cousin

If you've tried growing lychee in Florida, you already know it can be a challenge. The tree is beautiful and the fruit is exceptional, but lychee requires very specific conditions to produce reliably. Chill hours, drainage, and timing all have to line up just right, and even then, fruiting is never guaranteed.

Because of that, many Florida growers turn to longan. Longan is closely related to lychee and produces a very similar fruit with sweet, translucent flesh surrounding a dark seed. The difference is reliability. Longan tolerates Florida's climate far better, requires fewer chill hours, and fruits more consistently under typical home-garden conditions.

I am growing a lychee myself, but longan has earned its place as the more dependable option for gardeners who want that flavor profile without the uncertainty. For most Florida yards, longan delivers the experience people hope for when they plant lychee, with far less stress.

A Different Kind of Sweet

The flavor of a longan is sweet and musky, some say it tastes like a cross between a lychee and a grape. The texture is that same soft, almost jelly like feel that makes lychees so addictive. The best part? Longan produces in heavy clusters like grapes hanging from a tree. You do not pick one fruit at a time; you pick whole branches covered in fruit. If you want that tropical candy experience but you don't want to spend every winter stressed out over chill hours, longan is the way to go.

Why it works for Florida

Longan is just more adaptable. It handles our heat and humidity without complaining. Because it needs fewer chill hours than lychee, it fruits reliably even as far south as Miami, though it does great in Central Florida too. It is self fertile, so you only need one tree to get a massive harvest, and once it starts fruiting, it keeps going year after year. It is a workhorse for the food forest.

How to grow your own

From what I have learned, longan loves full sun and wants all the light it can get. You have to plant it in well draining soil because longan does not like to sit in water. If your soil is heavy, plant on a mound or mix in some sand and compost. You water it regularly when the tree is young and when it is flowering, but once it is established, it is fairly drought tolerant.

Mulch around the base to keep the roots cool and choose the right variety for your zone. If you are in South Florida, look for something like Kohala that does not need much chill. In Central Florida, you have a few more options. These trees can get big, thirty to forty feet, but you can keep them pruned to fifteen or twenty feet to keep things manageable. While mature trees can handle light frosts, you still need to protect those young trees from a hard freeze. Anything below 30°F can cause damage.

The Dragon Eye

In many cultures, longan is called the "Dragon Eye" because when you peel the skin and look at the translucent flesh with the dark seed inside, it looks just like an eye. My kids think that is the coolest thing ever. It turns a snack into a story. We eat them fresh by the handful, but you can also dry them or use them in desserts. They are high in vitamin C and antioxidants, making them a healthy, sweet treat that actually wants to grow in our backyard.

Toni's Tip

If you are like me and you just have to have a lychee, go for it, but plant a longan right next to it. That way, in those years when the lychee decides to be stubborn and skip a season, you'll still have clusters of "Dragon Eyes" to keep the kids happy. Give it a sunny spot, keep it pruned, and work with our Florida climate instead of fighting it.

55. Mamey Sapote

The Cuban Milkshake Tree

I first tasted mamey sapote at a Cuban restaurant in Miami. They had it on the menu as a milkshake—*Batido de mamey*.

I had no idea what it was, but the waiter looked at me and said, "You have to try it. It is the best." So I ordered it, and when it came out, it was this beautiful salmon pink color. It was thick, creamy, and sweet. I took one sip and I was hooked. It tasted like a sweet potato met a pumpkin pie and decided to become a milkshake. It had this rich, nutty flavor that was just incredible.

I asked the waiter what it was, and he told me, "Mamey. It is a fruit. Cubans go crazy for it." I started researching it and found out he wasn't kidding. Mamey sapote is a massive deal in Cuban and Caribbean communities for ice cream and smoothies. The flesh is dense, naturally sweet, and creamy enough that you barely need to add sugar. I knew right then I had to grow this. It is a true tropical gem that brings people back to their childhood with one sip.

Why it works for Florida

Mamey sapote loves our heat and humidity. It is a true tropical plant, so the warmer it gets, the better it grows. The fruit is large, usually four to six inches long, which means one fruit can make multiple milkshakes for the kids. Once it starts fruiting, it is a reliable producer. In South Florida, it is a staple, but even in Central Florida, you can make it work if you are willing to give it some extra care during our cold snaps.

How to grow and plant your own

From everything I have learned, mamey sapote wants full sun and all the light it can get. You need well draining soil because mamey does not like to sit in the muck. When you are ready to plant, dig a hole twice as wide as the root ball but no deeper. You want the top of the root ball to be level with or slightly above the ground. If you have heavy clay soil, build a small mound and plant the tree into that to ensure the water moves away from the trunk.

You water it regularly when the tree is young, but once it is established, it is surprisingly drought tolerant. Just remember that consistent water helps with fruit production later on. Mulch heavily around the base, but keep it a few inches away from the trunk, to keep those roots cool and protected.

Managing the cold and the size

The real challenge here is the cold. Mamey sapote is a heat lover. If you are in Central Florida like I am, you have to be ready to protect it. Young trees can be damaged by anything below 40°F. Mature trees can handle a brief dip into the mid 30s, but any colder than that and you risk losing the whole tree. It can also get huge, forty to sixty feet tall, so you will want to prune it to keep it around twenty feet if you want to be able to reach the fruit without a massive ladder.

The waiting game and the harvest

I am going to be real with you: mamey sapote is not for the impatient. It takes five to seven years before you get your first fruit from a grafted tree, and even longer from a seed. But once it starts, it is worth the wait.

Another thing to remember is that the fruit does not ripen on the tree. You have to pick it when it is mature but still hard, then let it sit on your counter for one to three weeks. You will know it is ready to pick when the skin looks slightly dull. A trick I learned is to scratch the skin near the stem; if the flesh underneath is orange or salmon colored, it is ready. If it is green, leave it alone. If you pick it too early, it will stay hard forever. If you wait too long on the tree, it will drop and split.

55. Mamey Sapote

In the kitchen

Fresh mamey is incredible just scooped out with a spoon, but the real star is that *Batido de mamey.* I blend the salmon colored flesh with milk, a little vanilla, and ice. It is thick, rich, and nostalgic. You can also make mamey ice cream or toss it into a smoothie. Just remember: the large seed inside is toxic, so scoop around it and toss it out.

Why it is good for you

This isn't just a treat; it is actually a powerhouse of nutrition.

- **High in Vitamins A and C:** Great for your immune system and your skin.
- **Packed with Fiber:** Supports healthy digestion.
- **Antioxidants:** Contains compounds that help fight inflammation.
- **Heart Health:** It is a good source of potassium and magnesium.

Toni's Tip

A tree that makes Cuban milkshakes is a tree worth waiting for. People will pay five to ten dollars for a single mamey at the market because the flavor is that unique. If you have the space and the patience, get one in the ground. I have picked my spot and I am ready to plant. It brings a piece of Caribbean history right into the backyard, and once you taste that first homemade batido, you will understand why people wait years for it.

Did You Know?

Mamey sapote is native to Central America and the Caribbean. It has been cultivated for centuries.

In Cuba and other Caribbean countries, mamey is a cultural staple. Batido de mamey is as common as orange juice.

The large seed inside the fruit is toxic. Do not eat it. Just scoop out the flesh around it.

56. Breadfruit

The Tree That Feeds a Village

I grew up hearing stories about breadfruit. My mom would talk about it like it was magic. One fruit could feed a whole family. You could roast it, boil it, fry it, or mash it. It tasted like bread when you cooked it, which is how it got the name. In Haiti and across the Caribbean, breadfruit is not just food. It is survival. It is the tree that feeds people when nothing else is available. One tree can produce hundreds of pounds of fruit per year, and each fruit can weigh five to ten pounds.

I have been wanting to plant breadfruit for years, but I kept putting it off because I heard it needs space. A lot of space. I was not sure if our yard could handle it. But then I saw a pattern starting to form. I am a huge fan of the Food Network, and there it was on *Chopped*. Watching those chefs scramble to figure out what to do with this massive, bumpy green fruit confirmed what my mom already knew: this thing is a powerhouse.

Then I saw a friend's tree producing in person. The fruit was massive. She picked one and we roasted it that afternoon. We sliced it thick, brushed it with oil, and roasted it until the outside was crispy and the inside was soft and starchy. It tasted like a cross between a potato and fresh baked bread. Mild, filling, and satisfying. I knew right then that I needed this tree.

Why it works for Florida

Breadfruit is a true tropical, so it loves our heat and humidity. One mature tree produces a staggering amount of food, sometimes hundreds of pounds a year. Because the fruit is so large, one single harvest can feed the whole family. It is versatile in the kitchen and deeply rooted in Caribbean tradition. It is history and survival in a single plant.

How to grow your own

From what I have learned, breadfruit needs full sun and lots of room to breathe. This tree gets big, sometimes forty to sixty feet tall and just as wide. You cannot plant it in a corner and expect it to stay small. It needs well draining soil because it does not like to sit in the muck.

You water regularly when the tree is young, and once it is established, it handles dry spells fairly well. Mulch heavily to keep the moisture in and the weeds out. Now, here is the reality check: breadfruit is best for South Florida. It does not handle cold well at all. Young trees can be damaged by temperatures below 50°F. If you are in Central Florida like me, you can try it, but you will need to protect it from cold snaps. If you are in North Florida, you would likely need a greenhouse to make it work.

The harvest and the kitchen

Breadfruit is ready to pick when the skin changes from bright green to a duller, yellowish green. You want to pick it when it is mature but still firm. Do not wait for it to soften on the tree or it will be overripe. When you cut it from the tree, wear gloves. The sap is a sticky white latex that will coat everything it touches.

In the kitchen, we love it roasted. You slice it thick, brush it with oil and salt, and roast it until it is crispy. You can also boil and mash it just like a potato with butter and garlic. In Haiti, it is often cooked in stews or served alongside meat and rice because it soaks up the flavors of whatever it is cooked with. It is naturally gluten free and high in fiber, making it a healthy, starchy staple.

The Chopped Challenge: Three Ways to Win with Breadfruit

If you were handed a basket with one breadfruit, here is how you would win the round:

- The Fried Appetizer: Thinly slice the breadfruit and fry it until it turns golden brown. Toss it in sea salt and lime zest. It is better than a potato chip and twice as filling.
- The Hearty Main: Boil chunks of breadfruit in salted water until tender, then sauté them with onions, garlic, and peppers. Serve it alongside some spicy jerk chicken or a rich Haitian legume stew.
- The Mashup: Mash the boiled breadfruit with butter, coconut milk, and fresh herbs. It has a creamy, tropical flavor that puts standard mashed potatoes to shame.

56. Breadfruit

Why it is good for you

- High in fiber: It keeps you full and supports digestion.
- Complex carbohydrates: This is slow burning energy that lasts.
- Nutrient dense: It is a great source of potassium, vitamin C, and magnesium.
- Naturally gluten free: A perfect starch replacement for almost any meal.

What no one tells you

- Space is non negotiable: This is a shade tree that produces food. Do not plant it if you do not have the room.
- Sticky business: The latex oozes from the fruit and the tree. Oil your knife and wear gloves when you harvest.
- Cold sensitivity: This tree does not forgive the cold. If you get regular freezes, this might not be the tree for you.

Where to Find These Plants & Keep Growing

Now that you have read through 50+ of my favorite plants and maybe even picked out a few for your own garden, let's talk about where you can actually get them. Knowing what to grow is one thing, but knowing where to find a healthy version that actually produces fruit is a whole other story.

Grafted Trees

If you want fruit fast, go grafted. These are already mature branches stuck onto strong rootstock, and they often fruit in one to two years. Grafted trees are great for mango, citrus, guava, loquat, and star fruit.

Where to find them:

- **Local nurseries:** Support them if you can! They know our local conditions best.
- **Florida growers on Etsy or Facebook Marketplace:** Just make sure you check those reviews first.
- **Fruit and Spice Park plant sales:** Keep an eye out for local rare fruit expos too.

Air Layered

Air layering gives you a clone of the exact tree, roots and all, right from a branch. They are often better for figs, mulberries, and lychee. They fruit a little quicker than seedlings but slower than grafted trees. You can visit our webpage at **Https://RootedinJs.com** to learn more about how to air layer, when to start, and which tropicals respond best to it.

Final Tip

When you are buying a plant, always ask these three things:

- **Was this grown in Florida?** If it was not, it might struggle with our humidity, pests, and sandy soil.
- **Is this grafted or seed grown?** This matters for timing and fruit quality.
- **Will it fruit in a pot?** If your space is limited, do not skip this question.

Where to Find These Plants & Keep Growing

You have got this. Whether you are growing in-ground, in pots, on a patio, or just starting with one plant on your balcony, you are rooted in something powerful. And if you ever need a little inspiration or want to see what is growing in my yard, come visit me online. I share my favorite tree purchases, new garden finds, and direct nursery links at **https://RootedinJs.com**

Now go grow something you love.

I will be out back picking mangoes… or wrestling a banana rhizome. *Bye…*

Florida Nursery Directory by Region

Finding the right tree is half the battle. If you are ready to get your hands dirty, here are some of the best places across Florida to find healthy, productive plants. These are the spots that know our soil and our "liquid sun" humidity.

Central Florida (Polk, Lake, Orange, and Hillsbrough)

This is our neck of the woods. These nurseries are great at providing varieties that can handle our slightly cooler winter nights while still thriving in the summer heat.

- **A Natural Farm (Howey-in-the-Hills):** A fantastic spot for organic edible plants, ginger, turmeric, and unique fruit trees.
- **Lukas Nursery (Oviedo):** A massive selection. They have a great butterfly encounter, but their fruit tree section is where the real treasure is.
- **Jene's Tropicals (St. Petersburg):** Technically on the coast, but a go-to for many Central Floridians looking for citrus and mangoes.
- **Eve's Garden Gifts (Land O' Lakes):** Great for those looking for smaller starts and unique succulents or indoor-to-outdoor transitions.

South Florida (Miami-Dade, Broward, and Palm Beach)

The tropical paradise. This is where you go for the heavy hitters like mamey sapote, breadfruit, and the ultra-tropical mangoes.

- **Fairchild Tropical Botanic Garden (Coral Gables):** Keep an eye on their plant sales. It is where you find the absolute rarest of the rare.
- **Pine Island Nursery (Miami):** One of the gold standards for grafted tropical fruit trees. If they don't have it, it might not exist in Florida.
- **Exotic Guava (Florida City):** Don't let the name fool you; they have an incredible variety of tropicals beyond just guava.
- **Top Tropicals (Fort Myers/Punta Gorda):** A huge online presence, but their physical locations are like walking through a jungle of edible options.

North Florida (Leon, Duval, and Alachua)

For my friends up north, you need "cold-hardy" champions. These nurseries specialize in plants that can handle a true frost.

- **Just Fruits and Exotics (Crawfordville):** This is the place for persimmons, figs, mulberries, and cold-hardy citrus. They are experts in North Florida growing.
- **Tallahassee Nurseries (Tallahassee):** A beautiful spot with a very knowledgeable staff that can help you pick the right variety for Zone 8.
- **Standard Feed & Seed (Jacksonville):** A classic spot for seeds, starters, and local advice that has been around for generations.

Online and Specialty Florida Growers

Sometimes you just want it delivered to your door. These Florida-based shops, as of 2026, are great for those of us who can't make the drive.

- **Sow Exotic (Winter Haven):** They ship beautiful, healthy edible plants all over the country and are right here in our backyard.
- **GreenDreams (Online/Central FL):** Pete Kanaris and his team are legends in the Florida food forest world. Great for permaculture-minded growers.
- **Etsy (Search for "Florida Grown"):** Just remember to check those reviews! There are some incredible small-scale backyard growers on here doing great work.

Acknowledgments

First and foremost, I thank God for the health, strength, and joy to plant, grow, and share these lessons with you.

To my four beautiful babies

You are the real Rooted in J's! You are the reason I can never go live... no one would hear me. I love our loud house. You are my little helpers, my taste testers, and my biggest reasons for growing food with love. You have taught me that patience, curiosity, and a willingness to get a little dirt under your nails are the best gardening tools of all.

To my husband, Jermaine

The other J, my motivation, and my T-post! You are the one who stays sturdy and holds everything up when things get crazy. You started out as my tree mover and somehow became more of a gardener than I am. You are the one I run every single crazy idea through, and the reason we are able to do all of this together. When I was pregnant and the Florida heat kept me inside, you said, "No worries, I got this." And you did. From carrying every shovel and planting every tree to being my sous chef—even if it isn't always by choice—thank you for helping turn our backyard into a food-filled oasis. I couldn't do this without you.

To my mommy

You are the reason I can transform these harvests into real Haitian meals that carry the flavors of home. Thank you for passing down traditions, recipes, and a love for food that feeds more than the body.

To my mother-in-law, Momma J

The container gardener expert in the north who is not afraid of a little cold. Thank you for your love, support, and everything you have poured into our family, helping me more than you will ever know.

To my father-in-law, Poppa J

You were so much more than my biggest cheerleader. I truly felt like more of your daughter than Jermaine was your birth son. I was so blessed to have a supporter like you, someone I could talk to about anything, knowing you were always there to listen. We miss you every single day, and I know the babies feel that void too. We planted a Valencia Pride mango tree in your honor because, just like you, it is strong and can take anything the world throws at it. Like you told me, "This is not goodbye... I will meet you in the garden."

To my dad

You planted the first seeds of knowledge in me. For every phone call that started with, "Here is what you need to do," your wisdom is rooted in these pages. You are a man of little words, but they are filled with wisdom and experience. Thank you for being my foundation.

To my extended family and friends

Thank you for cheering me on, sharing meals from our harvest, and encouraging me to keep going when the Florida heat tried to knock me down.

To my readers and my extended social family

Whether you are planting your first container garden or expanding your backyard into a full food forest, I hope this book inspires you to grow with confidence and joy. Thank you for letting my garden be part of your journey.

Glossary

Here is the quick breakdown of the terms I use around the yard and a cheat sheet for when you should be getting your hands in the dirt.

Air Layering A way to grow a whole new tree from a branch while it is still attached to the mama tree. You wrap a section of the branch in wet moss until it grows roots, then you cut it off and plant it. It is how I get exact clones of my favorite trees.

Annual A plant that completes its entire life cycle—seed, growth, flower, seed—in a single growing season. These must be replanted each year.

Calyx The outer casing of a flower bud. In Roselle (Florida Cranberry), this red part is the prize we harvest for teas, jams, and sauces.

Chill Hours The total number of hours the temperature stays below 45°F during the winter. This is the big reason why some trees, like certain lychees or peaches, struggle in Florida. They are waiting for a cold snap that never stays long enough.

Coco Coir A growing medium made from coconut husk fiber. It holds onto moisture while still allowing for good drainage. It is a great sustainable alternative to peat moss.

Compost Decomposed organic matter like food scraps and yard waste. We use this to feed the soil and improve its structure.

Deciduous These are the trees like figs and mulberries that will drop every single leaf in the winter. Don't panic when it happens—they are not dead, they are just sleeping.

Drought Tolerant This describes a plant that can handle the Florida heat without needing you to stand over it with a hose every five minutes. Once these are established, they can take a dry spell and keep on pushing.

Epis The heartbeat of Haitian cooking. It is a savory green seasoning paste made from blended peppers, garlic, herbs, and aromatics. It is the primary marinade and flavor base for almost everything I make.

Established This is the magic moment when a plant's roots have finally grown out of their original hole and into the surrounding soil. Once a tree is established, it is much tougher and does not need as much babying.

Evergreen A plant that keeps its green leaves all year round. Most of our tropical favorites, like the mango and sapodilla, are evergreens, meaning they do not leave your yard looking bare in the winter.

Food Forest A gardening style that mimics a natural forest but uses plants that you can actually eat. Instead of just rows of one thing, you have layers like tall fruit trees, smaller bushes, and ground covers all working together.

Grafted Plant A plant where a stem piece (scion) from one plant is joined to the roots (rootstock) of another. Grafted fruit trees typically produce earlier than seed grown trees.

Hardiness Zone A geographic classification based on average annual extreme minimum temperatures. Central Florida is primarily Zone 10a (30 to 35°F minimum).

Legim A classic, slow cooked Haitian eggplant stew. It is filled with vegetables and aromatics and is best served over rice and plantains.

Microclimate A small, localized area with climate conditions different from the surrounding region, such as a warm south facing wall or a cooler shaded corner.

Mulch A layer of organic material spread on soil to conserve moisture, regulate temperature, and enrich soil as it decomposes.

Mycorrhizae The good guys in the soil. These beneficial fungi form a relationship with plant roots and dramatically increase their ability to absorb water and nutrients.

N P K The three numbers you see on every bag of fertilizer. They stand for Nitrogen for green leaves, Phosphorus for roots and flowers, and Potassium for overall health and fruit quality.

Neem Oil A natural pesticide and fungicide pressed from neem tree seeds. It is a safe, organic way to handle insects and fungal diseases.

Nematode Microscopic roundworms in the soil. Root knot nematodes damage plant roots, but beneficial species actually prey on other soil pests.

Node A joint or bump on a plant stem where new leaves, branches, or roots can grow. This is essential to know if you are propagating by cuttings.

Perennial A plant that lives for more than two years, often dying back and regrowing each season. These are the long term residents of your food forest.

Perlite Lightweight white volcanic glass that improves drainage and keeps your potting mix from getting too packed down.

pH Soil A measure of how acidic or alkaline your soil is on a 0 to 14 scale. Most vegetables prefer a range of 6.0 to 7.0. Florida sandy soils tend to be slightly acidic.

Propagation Creating new plants from seeds, cuttings, divisions, air layering, or grafting.

Pup / Sucker A small offshoot growing from the base of a parent plant. Banana, aloe vera, and pineapple all produce pups that can be separated and replanted.

Rhizome A horizontal underground stem that spreads out and sends up shoots above and roots below. This is how ginger, turmeric, and bananas grow.

Root Bound A condition where roots have outgrown their container and are circling the pot walls. Signs include stunted growth and rapid wilting.

Sandy Soil The sugar sand we deal with here in Florida. It is great for drainage, but it does not hold onto water or nutrients very well, which is why we focus so much on mulch and compost.

Self Fertile This means the tree can produce fruit all by itself without needing a partner tree nearby for pollination. It is perfect for small yards.

Taproot The main, central root that grows straight down into the earth. It acts like an anchor for the tree and helps it find water deep underground.

Top Dressing When you add a layer of compost or fertilizer to the surface of the soil around a plant rather than digging it in. It lets the nutrients soak down naturally when it rains.

Worm Castings Earthworm excrement. It is one of the most nutrient rich, gentle natural fertilizers you can find.

Zone 10a / 10b The USDA Hardiness Zones covering most of Central and South Florida. Zone 10a has a minimum of 30 to 35°F, while Zone 10b ranges from 35 to 40°F.

Seasonal Planting Calendar

This is a general guide for Central Florida (Zone 10a). Remember that times will vary based on your specific microclimate and the year.

Spring (February - April)	Summer (May - August)	Fall (September - November)	Winter (December - January)
Papaya	Okra	Roselle (Florida Cranberry)	Lychee
Cassava	Sweet Potato	Callaloo / Amaranth	Longan
Pigeon Peas	Moringa	Loquat	Avocado
Sugarcane	Katuk	Mulberry	Mango
Lemongrass	Seminole Pumpkin	Guava	Jackfruit
Shampoo Ginger	Snake Gourd	Figs	Breadfruit
Dragon Fruit	Yardlong Beans	Citrus (best time to transplant)	Mamey Sapote
Passionfruit	Calabaza	Asparagus	Leaf of Life
Pineapple	Cranberry Hibiscus		Aloe Vera
Banana (pups)	Taro		
Okinawa Spinach			
Malabar Spinach			

References & Resources

[1] University of Florida IFAS Extension. Comprehensive guides for Florida gardeners. edis.ifas.ufl.edu

[2] USDA Plant Hardiness Zone Map. Find your hardiness zone. planthardiness.ars.usda.gov

[3] National Gardening Association. Plant databases and growing guides. garden.org

[4] The Old Farmer's Almanac. Planting calendars and frost dates. almanac.com

[5] Florida Dept. of Agriculture and Consumer Services. Plant regulations and pest alerts. fdacs.gov

[6] ChipDrop. Free wood chip delivery for home gardeners. chipdrop.com

[7] Hillsborough County — Rain Barrel Program. Free rain barrel distribution. Contact Hillsborough County Solid Waste for current availability.

[8] Jefferson, Jermaine. Grow Food NOT Lawns: Simple Steps to Turn Any Yard Into a Year-Round Garden. Growfitfl.com

[9] RootedinJs.com. Toni Jefferson's website: plant recommendations, nursery links, and exclusive reader content.

[10] Fuglie, L.J. (2001). The Miracle Tree: The Multiple Uses of Moringa. CWS, Dakar. [Moringa nutritional reference]

About the Author

Toni Jefferson is a Central Florida food forest gardener, author, and community educator who believes every family deserves fresh food grown with their own hands. Born and raised in Miami, Florida, Toni brings her Caribbean and Haitian heritage into the way she gardens, cooks, and teaches. For her, growing food is about more than the harvest. It is about memory, culture, and the stories shared around the dinner table.

What began in 2020 with a single watermelon seed quickly turned into a mission. Toni, her husband Jermaine, and their four children transformed their suburban yard in West Central Florida into a thriving backyard food forest. The garden was not built overnight. It grew through trial, mistakes, patience, and many seasons of learning what truly works in Florida soil.

Toni is the creator of the **30 Day Garden Challenge**, which has helped thousands of Florida gardeners discover plants that actually thrive in our unique climate. Her earlier guide, *30+ Plants That Won't Let You Down*, introduced gardeners to reliable crops for Florida yards. This book expands that list and dives deeper into the plants, lessons, and real world experience that shaped her garden.

Gardening is a shared mission in the Jefferson household. Toni and her husband Jermaine believe that productive gardens belong in everyday yards, not just farms. Jermaine is also an author whose books include *Grow Food NOT Lawns*, *Discipline: What Nobody Wants to Hear*, and *Florida's Perennial Garden*. Together they encourage families to turn ordinary spaces into living food forests.

Toni continues to share her garden journey, nursery discoveries, and practical growing advice through her website and community at **rootedinjs.com**. Readers can also explore Jermaine's books and garden resources at **growfitfl.com**.

Their goal is simple. Help more families grow real food, right where they are.

www.ingramcontent.com/pod-product-compliance
Ingram Content Group UK Ltd.
Pitfield, Milton Keynes, MK11 3LW, UK
UKHW050146280726
14058UKWH00007B/868

Want a thriving garden in the Sunshine State?

The Florida Grow List is your go-to guide for growing the tastiest, easiest, and most reliable plants for Florida's unique climate. Whethe you're new to gardening or just looking to improve your harvests, thi book makes it simple to grow delicious, heat-loving food right in Florida soil.

Inside you'll discover

- 50+ plants that thrive in Florida's heat and humidity
- The best times to plant, harvest, and care for each crop
- Simple, straightforward tips without confusing gardening jargon

From tropical favorites like sweet potatoes, papayas, and dragon frui to backyard staples like moringa and sugarcane, this book is packed with plants that actually want to grow in Florida.

If you're ready to spend less time guessing and more time harvesting, The Florida Grow List will help you build a productive, resilient garde that thrives in the Sunshine State.

Connect online @rootedinjs.com for tips, updates, and a supportive Florida gardening community.